IGNATIUS
SANCHO

Front cover
Ignatius Sancho, 1729–1780
By Thomas Gainsborough, 1768 (detail)
Oil on canvas, 96.5 x 84.5 cm
© National Gallery of Canada, Ottawa

Back cover
Ignatius Sancho, 1729–1780
By Thomas Gainsborough, 1768 (full image)
Oil on canvas, 96.5 x 84.5 cm
© National Gallery of Canada, Ottawa

IGNATIUS SANCHO

AN AFRICAN MAN OF LETTERS

REYAHN KING

SUKHDEV SANDHU

JAMES WALVIN

JANE GIRDHAM

Foreword by Caryl Phillips

Published in Great Britain by
National Portrait Gallery Publications,
National Portrait Gallery, St Martin's Place,
London WC2H 0HE

ISBN 1 85514 192 2

A catalogue record for this book is available
from the British Library

Contents

The idea of 'the man of taste' is a familiar one in all accounts of 18th-century aesthetics. Indeed, it is an idea which is central to the received notion of 18th-century society and has subsequently acquired negative connotations, suggesting a broad, but not deep, culture which created a common culture of politeness at the level of the aristocracy and the urban gentry, but which was at the same time deliberately and intentionally exclusive.

However any notion that 18th-century culture was monolithic is currently being undermined by a great range of studies by social historians, art historians and historians of ideas. It is now normal in any study of the 18th century to pay much closer attention to its commercial character, examining the ways in which conventions of politeness might just be a means of marketing goods and the ways in which debates over aesthetics might act as a masquerade for social change and political dispute.

It is in the light of such arguments over the nature of 18th-century society that it is fascinating to read of Ignatius Sancho, 'a coal-black, jolly African' as he described himself, who was also a man of taste. Born on a slave ship half way across the Atlantic, he subsequently became a valet, a writer in the popular periodicals of his day, a musician, a Methodist and a grocer. His life enriches and diversifies one's sense of what was possible (and, indeed, what was not possible) in 18th-century life as he moves from being a servant to the Duchess of Montagu, to becoming a correspondent with Laurence Sterne, a sitter to Thomas Gainsborough and a friend of David Garrick; and his career makes it possible to look at the underside of polite society and the ways in which it was in an individual's interests to subscribe to its conventions.

This book has emerged from an exhibition, which is due to be held at the National Portrait Gallery from 24 January to 11 May 1997. It gives the research which has gone into the exhibition a more permanent form and it is intended that the book should itself be a contribution to the increasing literature of black studies. I am delighted that it has been possible to publish the book under the Gallery's expanding publishing programme and I hope that it will be seen as part of the Gallery's commitment to the support of new academic research. I would like at the same time to acknowledge the help that we have received for the exhibition from Booker PLC through Jonathan Taylor, its chairman and a member of our development board, and also from British Airways who have made it possible for us to borrow the portrait of Sancho from the National Gallery of Canada, Ottawa.

Charles Saumarez Smith
Director, National Portrait Gallery

The second half of the 20th century has witnessed the decline of Britain as a power of global significance. Concomitant with this waning of international importance has been a redefinition of what it means to be British. In the 1960s, comments by the Tory MP Enoch Powell, which sought to exclude black people from the national picture, reminded the populous that Britain possessed a racially-constructed concept of nation. In the 1980s, with the emergence of a second generation of black people who were born in Britain, Mrs Thatcher redefined this concept to actually *include* some black people. However, this redefinition of nation was not a benevolent act. Mrs Thatcher's 'generosity' was directly connected to Britain's increasing sense of herself as somehow inadequate. In the 1980s and early 1990s, Poll Tax rioters, Clause 28 'Queers', Brussels Bureaucrats, and the perpetrators of 'race' riots, all fed Britain's sense of herself as a nation in crisis. There was a perceived need to co-opt 'trouble-makers' from the fringes, and make them feel a part of the centre. What Mrs Thatcher achieved by including black people into her concept of nation was to introduce the idea of divide and rule into the domestic arena, an idea which had long been used as a central tenet of empire.

In 1983 the Conservative Party produced, with the aid of the advertising firm Saatchi and Saatchi, a now notorious election poster. It featured a black man who was smartly dressed in a suit and carrying a briefcase. The caption read: 'Labour says he's black. Tories say he's British.' Implicit in the new Thatcherite concept of nationhood was the idea that one could not be both black and British. Black equals bad, British equals good. We will take you as British as long as you look like you belong – no afros, no dashikis, no beads, no shoulder bags, only a suit, tie and briefcase thank you very much. For the first time in British history, two types of black person were now being officially recognised: the 'good' and the 'bad' – the British and the black, the assimilable and the subversive. The nation had certainly moved on from the 'Powellite' model in which *all* blacks were to be excluded from the national narrative and encouraged to go 'back to where they came from'.

Two hundred years ago, toward the end of the 18th century, Georgian England was fast approaching a crossroads. The times were still characterised by leisure: slow wagons, pedlars in the street, spinning-wheels, but already one could detect the strains of the industrial age that would quickly eradicate this bucolic Hanoverian era. England was beginning to be troubled by political disturbances such as the Gordon Riots. As if this were not enough, there was also a deeply-ingrained fear of Catholicism and Irish immigration and an open acknowledgement of the nuisance of free blacks and slaves who occupied both high and low stations in national life. Generally, there was a recognised confusion as to how this great nation might now comport itself on the threshold of modern times. There was no need to espouse a racially-constructed nationalism, for it was understood that the nation was white and that the black presence, no matter how annoying and unseemly, posed no real threat for it simply represented the unwelcome backwash of the nation's maritime adventures in the slave trade. The thousands of blacks, who congregated in Liverpool, Bristol and London, constituted a 'problem' that might be solved by such practical means as the founding of the colony of Sierra Leone and, if necessary, the wholescale deportation of the dark strangers.

Two hundred years later, despite the Powellite cry to send them 'back to where they came from', Britain's black population are clearly a more permanent part of the national scene. The cultural impact of black people on British society has been considerable, and it is this cultural 'work' which has helped to move the nation from the Powellite notion of exclusion toward the Thatcherite model of limited inclusion. Musical groups such as Aswad and Soul II Soul have exerted a powerful pull on the British sensibility – both black and white – not just in terms of music, but also in terms of style. In literature, the emergence of writers such as Salman Rushdie and Linton Kwesi Johnson meant that questions would inevitably have to be asked about what constitutes the nature of being British. After all, Linford Christie, Frank Bruno and Ian Wright, to name a few, have become national heroes, which means that Britain can no longer pretend to define her sense of nationality along strictly racial lines. These developments in the broadly 'cultural' zone have not been matched by similar developments in politics, business or government. The handful of black MPs that have begun to be elected, suggests that black people have only just started to gain a foothold on the lower rungs of 'power'. Clearly the changing racial definition of nation owes nearly everything to the cultural response.

In the 18th century there was certainly a cultural response to Britain by the black community in terms of music, literature and the theatre. Black musicians and actors populated the land, and writers such as Olaudah Equiano and Ukawsaw Gronniosaw spoke eloquently and forcefully about their individual lives and the general nature of the black experience in Britain. However, while the odd musician such as George Bridgetower may have been outstanding, there was not enough evidence of excellence in the work of these artists to force British society to sit up and take notice. One also has to bear in mind the fact that during this period it was difficult for a British black person to gain information regarding developments in the diaspora. Two hundred years later the black community in Britain would gain some confidence by observing the processes of decolonisation in Africa and the success of the Civil Rights movement in the United States. They were able to view their own interventions as part of a global stategy, whereas black people in 18th-century Britain largely perceived of their own efforts as occurring in a national context.

Ignatius Sancho started life on a slave ship in the mid-Atlantic. He arrived in England aged two, finding himself in the austere household of three sisters in Greenwich. Yet from these unpromising beginnings, Sancho went on to become a servant in the Duke of Montagu's household, a move which provided him with the opportunities to pursue an education and finally to leave service and open up his own grocery in London's Mayfair. It was then that Sancho became a dedicated correspondent. A devoted husband to a black West Indian wife, Anne Osborne, and father to six children, most of Sancho's letters concern the domestic travails of a grocer in ill-health trying to keep together body and soul. However, Sancho also feels moved to comment upon both political and literary life in Britain, and he does so with a deep love of the country and a thwarted desire to belong. In one particularly telling description he appropriates a Shakespearian image and then undermines it with the reality of his own appearance: 'Figure to yourself, my dear Sir, a man of a convexity of belly exceeding Falstaff – and a black face into the bargain.'

It is easy to think of Sancho as obsequious, but such a description is far too reductive. True enough, Sancho adopts a deferential tone in his dealings with society, but the same could be said of nearly every 'novice' writer of the period. It was common practice to display a full command of etiquette and to bow 'excessively' before one's literary and social superiors. In this sense Sancho was merely acknowledging the convention of the times. Although writing at the height of the debate about slavery, Sancho chose not to rail and preach against the evils of the institution in as outgoing a manner as say, Equiano. He did, however, bring up this very subject in his first letter to Laurence Sterne, encouraging the famous writer to wield his pen on the side of those lobbying for the abolition of the slave trade, ' – That subject, handled in your striking manner, would ease the yoke (perhaps) of many – but if only of one – Gracious God! – what a feast to a benevolent heart!'

To view this family man as an 'Uncle Tom' is to misread both the historical period and the nature of the man. The journey from slave ship to Mayfair shop is a remarkable one. Ignatius Sancho was hyper-conscious of his unique role in London society, providing as he did an alternative mirror into which one might peer and spy a black man beyond the model of the stage fool as perfected by such vagrants as Billy Waters, or the protester and pamphleteer such as Equiano and others. Sancho probably regarded himself as something of a role model, and his very presence in literary London would certainly have complicated many individual's ideas of blackness. In fact, a review of the first edition of the *Letters of The Late Ignatius Sancho* (1782), claimed that the book 'presents to us the naked effusions of a negroe's heart, and shews it glowing with the finest philanthropy, and the purest affections'. Sancho's dignity and literacy were never going to be enough to force British society to reconsider the model of a racially-constructed nation, but Sancho was the forerunner of the possibility of thinking about black people in assimilationist terms. He was a 'good' black.

The sociologist, Stuart Hall has recently noted the extent to which American academics and scholars of the African diasporan world are turning their attention towards both contemporary and historical Britain. It seems to me that this is largely because Britain provides the earliest model of vigorous interaction between those of the African diaspora and those of European origin. For much of the 18th century America remained a colony of Britain and her relationship with her black population was not as complex as Britain's, where a black middle class had clearly begun to emerge. However, this black British middle class was only able to negotiate 18th-century society with some difficulty. The personal anxieties of such negotiations resulted in the development of a 'double consciousness' along the lines which the great American philosopher and writer, W.E.B. Du Bois would later identify in the United States. There was among these pioneering black Britons a sense of both belonging and not belonging, a sense of being part of the nation and being outside of it. It is no wonder that in order to understand the roots of their own African diasporan traditions Americans have begun to look at Britain.

Ignatius Sancho held the key to understanding British society through both his command of the language and his bearing. However, by virtue of his pigmentation and history, he was doomed to occupy a role both 'central' *and* 'peripheral'. In contemporary Britain, Lord Taylor, a Tory member of the House of Lords, who has recently had to settle for a seat in the upper house after being spectacularly defeated in the 'safe' Tory seat of Cheltenham, represents the idea of a British black man who occupies both the centre and the margin. Such 'doubly-conscious' men are the true successors to Sancho, but their lives are made considerably easier in societies which are now happy to subscribe to assimilationist strategies of nationhood. While these 'Uncle Toms' will never win the general applause of 'the people', or disrupt the nation's sense of race, they will, by virtue of their very existence, ask the society to address itself to uncomfortable questions. What makes Ignatius Sancho's role in this strategy so intriguing, is that while the British nation was still mired in a guilt-free sense of itself as strictly white, and while there was an absence of cultural or political pressure to encourage the nation to adapt its image of itself, and while there was precious little reflected evidence of diasporan success beyond the shores of Britain, Sancho still persisted in ploughing his own unique 'doubly-conscious' furrow with a courageous dignity.

Caryl Phillips
London, December 1996

Chapter 1

Ignatius Sancho and Portraits of the Black Élite

Reyahn King

Sancho may be styled – what is very uncommon for men of his complexion, *A Man of Letters*

(*The Monthly Review*, 1783, pp. 492–7).

The 18th-century reviewer of *Letters of the late Ignatius Sancho, an African, To which are prefixed, Memoirs of his Life* clearly articulated contemporary opinion when he called Ignatius Sancho a man of letters. Although by the 19th century Sancho was considered a curiosity because of his colour, he had enjoyed the reputation of a man of letters and a man of taste amongst many of his contemporaries. Sentimental but knowing, Sancho's letters written in the later part of his life reveal an amiable, well-read man whose good humour prevailed against poverty, sickness and death. Sancho's wit was always combined with an elaborate courtesy, softening any ironic blows, and in the midst of family and financial concerns, he attempted to retain both Shandean mockery and religious faith. Luck and his ability to attract aristocratic patronage, to charm the fashionable world and earn for himself a respectable niche within London's artistic circles, ensured for Sancho not only a life of comparative comfort but also allowed his character and inclinations full rein in a way normally impossible for black men in British 18th-century society.

Most black men in 18th-century England arrived as slaves and their status and income, if any, usually reflected the disadvantage of their colour within an economic and social system reliant on slavery's products. Sancho and his friend Julius Soubise enjoyed the benevolent patronage of aristocratic families but they were exceptionally lucky, as Sancho emphasised in his letters to Soubise:

Happy, happy lad! what a fortune is thine! – Look round upon the miserable fate of almost all of our unfortunate colour – superadded to ignorance, – see slavery, and the contempt of those very wretches who roll in affluence from our labours. Superadded to this

> woeful catalogue – hear the ill-bred and heart-racking
> abuse of the foolish vulgar

(Edwards and Rewt, 1994, p. 56).

Although men like Sancho and Soubise were indeed
uncommon, they were representative of a small élite in
Britain's 18th-century black community. Portraits usually
indicate status and the few that are known or were
recorded of black people at this time include Sancho by
Gainsborough, the gallant swordsman Chevalier de Saint-
Georges, the missionary Philip Quaque, and formerly
enslaved Prince Job Ben Solomon. The surviving portraits
suggest a historical black community with varied skills
and experience, of which Sancho was undoubtedly a
member. Sancho assumed the role of moral mentor to
others in the community including Soubise and married a
black West Indian Anne Osborne. His musical friends
included Charles Lincoln, a black regimental musician who,
in Sancho's words, 'intends trying his fortune amongst us –
as teacher of murder & neck breaking – alias – fencing &
riding – ' (Edwards and Rewt, 1994, p. 62–3. Annotation
on original suggests 'My friend L — 'is Lincoln). Sancho
was always willing to attempt to find employment for other
colonial servants and to participate in the finding of
financial support for members of his community.

This chapter introduces Ignatius Sancho and his role
as a man of taste and letters in London's artistic circles. It
describes his portrait by Gainsborough and notes the
unusual quality of such a gentlemanly and well-painted
image of a black man in 18th-century England. It surveys
other members of Britain's black élite of the time and
discusses some of the most significant surviving 18th-
century portraits of Africans in Britain.

The book as a whole presents the different aspects of
Sancho's life – his interest in the arts, literary activities and
letter-writing, slavery and his role in abolition, his music
and other black musicians – in separate chapters which set

his experience against the background of black and white
societies in the 18th century.

Sukhdev Sandhu's chapter places Sancho's letters within
the context of writing by and about black people in
London. He discusses Sancho's letters in detail, particularly
in relation to Laurence Sterne. Unlike previous
commentators on Sancho's style, Sandhu does not read
Sancho's use of 'dashes, digressions and textual games' as
merely emulative. Instead he analyses them in relation to
the ironies and byways of Sancho's own life. Sandhu's
account of Sancho's letters demonstrates their familial
charm and movingly personal nature.

James Walvin's chapter provides the contemporary
context of slavery which better enables us to understand
the limitations imposed on Sancho. He demonstrates the
everyday, unavoidable nature of British imperial commerce
whether it was in sugar, tobacco or human cargo. Sancho's
life coincided with a period when the English legal position
on slavery was both changing and ambiguous. Walvin
outlines the beginnings of anti-slavery agitation and
analyses Sancho's contribution to the movement that
eventually achieved abolition of the slave trade.

Sancho's musical skills were fairly typical of more
successful black men, even those, like Olaudah Equiano
who played the french horn, whose energies and interests
were professionally directed elsewhere. Jane Girdham
summarises the careers of black professional musicians
George Augustus Polgreen Bridgetower, the Chevalier de
Saint-Georges and Joseph Antonia Emidy. She provides an
account of the many unknown black musicians who made
a lasting contribution to British music, especially through
Janissary military bands. Sancho's friend Charles Lincoln
was just one of those black regimental musicians, whilst his
brother-in-law John Osborne also worked in the military
and may well have played in a regimental band. Girdham
provides an introduction to Sancho's music and explains
the social use of his compositions. Examples of Sancho's
compositions, including the song 'Sweetest Bard', composed

to an ode by David Garrick, are reproduced amongst the illustrations.

These chapters demonstrate the range of Sancho's skills and the talent with which he developed his dilettante activities. Considering these interests against the context of others in the black community provides a picture of a small but multi-talented group of African men and women making their way with relative degrees of comfort through British 18th-century urban society.

Sancho's beginnings were inauspicious. He was born on a slave ship crossing the Atlantic and was baptised at Cartagena in Spanish America. Following the death of his mother and the suicide of his father, Sancho was brought to England at about two years old. He was given to three sisters in Greenwich who resisted his attempts to learn to read, judging that education would make him restive. He was deeply unhappy in his situation as a slave-servant in Greenwich. A hint of this is given many years later in his first letter to Laurence Sterne:

> The first part of my life was rather unlucky, as I was placed in a family who judged ignorance the best and only security for obedience. – A little reading and writing I got by unwearied application. – The latter part of my life has been – thro' God's blessing, more fortunate

> (Edwards and Rewt, 1994, p. 85).

Although Sancho couched the description of his unhappiness in terms of being withheld from education, his first biographer Joseph Jekyll, writing in 1782, suggested that Sancho's causes for distress were more wide-ranging. His mistresses apparently threatened to send him back to the West Indies, where slavery on the plantations was much harsher than the life of a 'pet' in London, and they restricted his social life.

John, 2nd Duke of Montagu, who owned Caribbean estates and had attempted to develop sugar plantations in St Lucia, had a residence on Blackheath, where he had seen and taken an interest in Sancho from an early age. According to Jekyll, he had 'brought him frequently home to the Duchess, indulged his turn for reading with presents of books, and strongly recommended to his mistresses the duty of cultivating a genius of such apparent fertility'. The 'cultivating of genius' was something of a hobby of the Duke's and long before meeting Sancho, he had paid for the education of the Jamaican slave Francis Williams at Cambridge. Although the Duke had died, Sancho fled in 1749 to the Duchess who, however, rebuffed him. He then threatened to commmit suicide and the Duchess relented, admitting him into her household as butler in 1749 or 1750. The speed with which he became a significant member of the Montagu household is surprising. The Duchess of Montagu died in 1751 and left Sancho a legacy of £70 and an annuity of £30. Such a legacy was unusually large for a servant of only two years' standing and although the size of the legacy probably also reflects the great wealth of the Montagu family, it demonstrates Sancho's status as an upper servant. Records of payments from 1752 to 1771 show that the subsistence annuity was indeed paid regularly every six months by the Duchess's heir, Mary Montagu (Countess of Cardigan, and later Duchess of Montagu), for the remainder of Sancho's life.*

Jekyll stated that Sancho squandered his legacy on women and gambling but however profligate he may have been, it was during this next stage of his life that he probably formed his friendships with people in the theatrical world. He adored the theatre and, according to Jekyll, spent his last shilling on a performance by Garrick of Richard III. He considered acting in the obvious roles of Oroonoko and Othello but a speech defect made the venture impossible. A decade or more later, Garrick and the actress Catherine Horneck (Mrs Bunbury) were still amongst his friends. In 1779 Sancho described a visit to the

---

* *Lady Cardigan's Account from 7 July 1749 to 10 July, 1755 and The Dutchess of Montagu's Account from 17 July 1769 to 22 July, 177–*, Boughton House Archive. (Other evidence relating to Sancho's position within the Montagu household will be published together with information relevant to Gainsborough's portrait of Sancho in a forthcoming article. For further information, please contact the publishers of this book.)

theatre in order to see another friend, John Henderson, playing Richard III. Loyal to Garrick with whom he had supper on the same evening, Sancho described the event:

> It was a daring undertaking – and Henderson was really awed with the idea of the great man, whose very robes he was to wear – and whose throne he was to usurp. – But give him his due – he acquitted himself well – tolerably well – He will play it much better next time – and the next better still. Rome was not built in six weeks – and, trust me, a Garrick will not be formed under seven years

> (Edwards and Rewt, 1994, p. 193).

By 1758 Sancho was back in service to the Montagu family. He married Anne Osborne on 17 December. George Brudenell, 4th Earl of Cardigan (son-in-law to the 2nd Duke of Montagu and later created Duke of Montagu himself), 'soon placed him about his person', probably as one of his valets (Edwards and Rewt, 1994, p. 23). Someone chosen for this role attended to the fashionable appearance of his master, occasionally acted as travelling companion and was expected to behave like a gentleman. Although Sancho's ill health and marriage puts the extent of his usefulness into some doubt, he was suited for such an honorific position. His skin colour alone made him an exotic asset and Sancho's personal qualities of intelligence and wit would have reflected well on his master. As an upper servant close to a personage as grand as the Earl of Cardigan, Sancho's position would have furthered his natural ability to befriend society figures. In turn, Sancho was loyal and grateful to the Montagu family whose patronage and support lasted throughout his life. In addition to encouragement, employment and the annuity, connection to the Montagu family ensured that Sancho and his large family received smaller practical benefits. Thus, the Earl of Cardigan paid five pounds and five shillings for

21

the christening of Sancho's eldest daughter Frances on 23 January, 1761 (George Cardigan's Account Books, 1755–1772 (NCRO, X4573)).

Sancho led a peripatetic life centred on his master's routine but he had ample opportunity in the Montagu household to develop his taste for art, literature and music as he came into contact with members of the family and their circle, who were art enthusiasts, collectors and amateur musicians. The dedications of the surviving works of Sancho's music are all to members of the Montagu family and he was able to produce and publish musical works whilst still a servant. His *Theory of Music* has been lost but volumes of songs, dances and music for the harpsichord survive. He became widely known as a man of letters following the publication of the letter which he sent to Laurence Sterne in 1766. Despite still being in service to the Montagu family, Sancho's literary reputation developed from this period.

By 1773, Sancho's gout and asthma necessitated retirement from service so he decided to set up a grocery. He shared his thoughts about the venture with Mrs H. —

> As soon as we can get a bit of house, we shall begin to look sharp for a bit of bread – I have strong hope – the more children, the more blessings – and if it please the Almighty to spare me from the gout, I verily think the happiest part of my life is to come – Soap, starch, and blue, with raisins, figs, &c. – we shall cut a respectable figure – in our printed cards

> (Edwards and Rewt, 1994, p. 59).

Despite the gout, Sancho was indeed happy as an independent family man. He wrote frequently to friends and correspondents sharing his enjoyment of literature, family life and politics. As a shopkeeper, Sancho seems to have become truly free to correspond and socialise with friends, artists and literary figures. Callers to his shop included aristocrats and patrons choosing to express their condescending support for this remarkable black man by buying his products, as well as those like George Cumberland who genuinely sought out the opinion of a man of letters.

Through ill-health and financial problems, Sancho's active interest in the arts and the world around him remained undimmed. Sancho's later letters to his friend, the Bury St Edmunds banker, John Spink, provide a lively account of contemporary events and politics in London. He described the Gordon Riots:

> There is at this present moment at least a hundred thousand poor, miserable, ragged rabble, from twelve to sixty years of age, with blue cockades in their hats...ready for any and every mischief. – Gracious God! what's the matter now? I was obliged to leave off – the shouts of the mob – the horrid clashing of swords – and the clutter of a multitude in swiftest motion – drew me to the door – when every one in the street was employed in shutting up shop

> (Edwards and Rewt, 1994, p. 231).

In his postscript he added:

> The Sardinian ambassador offered 500 guineas to the rabble to save a painting of our Saviour from the flames, and 1000 guineas not to destroy an exceeding fine organ: The gentry told him, they would burn him if they could get at him, and destroyed the picture and organ directly. – I am not sorry I was born in Afric

> (Edwards and Rewt, 1994, p. 232).

Sancho clearly enjoyed describing the exciting events and mocks his own voyeurism when he should have been shutting up shop like his neighbours. On the other hand, he disapproved of the violence and thoughtless iconoclasm not only because of the threat to property, law and order but also because he favoured toleration. The Gordon Riots were an expression of anti-Catholic and anti-Irish prejudice which Sancho would have opposed, as he did most prejudices. Looking back to the days of the riots, Sancho wrote 'Our religion has swallowed up our charity – and the fell daemon Persecution is become the sacred idol of the once free, enlightened, generous Britons.' Shopkeeper, property owner, voter and defender of culture though he was, Sancho had to withstand the assumption that he was a barbarian because he was of African origin. The Gordon Riots demonstrated that barbarity was not special to Africa and by juxtaposing the irrelevant detail of his pride in African descent against his account of the rabble, Sancho reminded his reader of the unjust and ridiculous nature of racial prejudice.

Sancho's 'retirement' to his shop in Charles Street had been occasioned by infirmity but it is only from November 1780 that his letters regularly recount the physical torments of his illnesses and mention a variety of doctors. Sancho's final letter to John Spink was dated 7 December 1780 and admitted that 'In good truth, I have been exceeding ill.' (Edwards and Rewt, 1994, p. 259). He died a week later on 14 December 1780, receiving a short obituary in the *Gentleman's Magazine*.

The opening lines of Sancho's famous introductory letter to Sterne appeals to sentiment via a shocking reference to his own position: 'Reverend Sir – It would be an insult (or perhaps look like it) to apologise for the liberty I am taking. – I am one of those people whom the vulgar and illiberal call '*Negurs*.' (Edwards and Rewt, 1994, p. 85). This letter paved the way to friendship with Sterne, for whom Sancho obtained a subscription from the Montagus for the ninth volume of *Tristram Shandy* and regularly called on at his lodgings.

Sancho learnt the perfect form of manners as a valet and sometimes appeared to rest all the thanks for his comparatively privileged position at the feet of his patrons and generous friends. Yet his angry comments about the status of American poet Phillis Wheatley suggest that he was not so obsequious as has sometimes been claimed: 'It reflects nothing either to the glory or generosity of her master – if she is still his slave – except he glories in the *low vanity* of having in his wanton power a mind animated by Heaven – a genius superior to himself.' (Edwards and Rewt, 1994, p. 122). Sancho chose to play the part of the educated man with a full command of etiquette who could appeal to the sentimentality of Sterne's generation in his attempts to highlight the injustices done to his fellow Africans. However, Sancho's reputation as a man of letters extended beyond his friendship and correspondence with Sterne or the novelty of an African literate and fluent in English. Although most of his letters were personal, some of them appeared in periodical literature during his lifetime and, as was common practice at the time, a few were written expressly for that purpose. Thus, he contributed for *The General Advertiser* a comical proposition to raise a regiment of hairdressers 'which are happily half-trained already for the service of their country by being – *powder proof* – ' (Edwards and Rewt, 1994, p. 225). In 1779 Edmund Rack requested Sancho's permission to publish two of his letters in a planned collection to be called *Letters of Friendship*. Sancho's two plays are now lost but they would have been known about by his contemporaries. The literary judgements expressed in Sancho's letters are confident and his critical opinion was valued and sought after. Aspiring author George Cumberland wrote to Richard Dennison Cumberland:

a black man, Ignatius Sancho, has lately put me into unbounded conceit with myself – he is said to be a great Judge of literary performances (God send it may be true!) and has praised my Tale of Cambambo, and

> Journal which I read to him, so highly that I shall like
> him as I live
>
> (BM Add Mss., 36, 514, f. 29).

In an animated letter to his close friend George Meheux,
Sancho wrote:

> give Tom Jones a second *fair* reading! – Fielding's wit is
> obvious – his humour poignant – dialogue just – and
> truly dramatic – colouring quite nature – and keeping
> chaste. – Sterne equals him in every thing, and in one
> thing excels him and all mankind – which is the
> distribution of his lights, which he has so artfully
> varied throughout his work, that the oftener they are
> examined the more beautiful they appear. – They were
> two great masters, who painted for posterity – and, I
> prophesy, will charm to the end of the English speech
>
> (Edwards and Rewt, 1994, p. 136).

Analogies with painting are clear in Sancho's choice of
words and, like other critics including Dr Johnson, Sancho
here judged literature according to the author's ability to
conjure a picture in the mind.

Sancho also enjoyed playing the role of literary guide.
Thus, he advised Jack Wingrave to 'preserve about 20 l. a
year for two or three seasons – by which means you may
gradually form a useful, elegant, little library –'. Amongst
Sancho's recommended volumes for the fledgling library
were 'a little of Geography – History –' (Robertson and
Goldsmith), two small volumes of Sermons by the
'dissenting minister' Mr Williams, 'Spectators – Guardians
– and Tatlers – you have of course. – Young's Night-
Thoughts – Milton – and Thomson's Seasons were my
summer companions for near twenty years –' (Edwards and
Rewt, 1994, p. 140).

In his letter to John Spink describing the Gordon Riots,
Sancho revealed his concern for the preservation of

beautiful objects, but he was equally interested in contemporary artists and their productions. In 1774 he reported to William Stevenson on the activities of John James Barralet and the drawing school set up by the Free Society of Artists (Sunderland, 1986, p. 28): 'I suppose you know he has opened an Academy in St. Alban's Street – at two guineas a year – naked figures three nights a week – '. Artists sought out Sancho in his shop and made calls on him there. J. T. Smith described a visit he paid to the shop in Charles Street with the sculptor Nollekens: 'as we pushed the wicket door, a little tinkling bell, the usual appendage to such shops, announced its opening: we drank tea with Sancho and his black lady, who was seated, when we entered, in the corner of the shop, chopping sugar, surrounded by her little "Sanchonets".'(Smith, 1828, pp. 27–8). Sancho was intimate with professional artists Daniel Gardner, John Hamilton Mortimer and the Norwich painter and miniaturist William Stevenson. An acquaintance of Richard Payne Knight, Sancho's ability as a connoisseur was recognised by J. T. Smith (Smith, 1829, p. 28) as well as by Joseph Jekyll who commented that 'Painting was so much within the circle of Ignatius Sancho's judgment and criticism, that Mortimer came often to consult him.'

Sancho hung a portrait of his friend Mrs Cocksedge, later Lady Bunbury, by Daniel Gardner above his chimney piece and Nollekens's gift of a plaster cast after his bust of Sterne (Figure 1) occasioned the visit described by Smith above. Besides these gifts, he owned a portrait of himself by Gainsborough. It is likely that he owned prints or other works by John Hamilton Mortimer and William Stevenson, an antiquarian whose work as an artist is now scarcely known but who was one of Sancho's most frequent correspondents. Sancho procured prints by Mortimer, and probably other artists, for friends and he commented on, and circulated, drawings and caricatures (for examples see letters 65 and 110). The immensely popular amateur artist Henry William Bunbury married Sancho's theatrical friend

Catherine Horneck. Bunbury later supplied a vignette for an additional title page to the fifth edition of Sancho's *Letters* published by William Sancho.

In his portrait of Sancho (see back cover), Gainsborough has committed to posterity a visual image which, like Sancho's *Letters,* is notably vivacious and shifting in mood. Sancho's expression seems both amused and quizzical as if Gainsborough has captured him on the verge of speech or laughter. Appropriately, a stipple engraving of 1781 by Bartolozzi after Gainsborough's portrait was used for the frontispiece of the posthumous edition of his *Letters.* Although excited by public life, Sancho was a family man who asserted domestic virtues above more public values. It does not surprise, therefore, that Gainsborough, whose supreme skill as a painter elevated domestic charm, produced an image so in keeping with Sancho's character. Gainsborough's skill is clearest in his treatment of Sancho's skin colour. Unlike Hogarth, whose use of violet pigments when painting black faces results in a greyish skin tone, the brick-red of Sancho's waistcoat in Gainsborough's portrait, combined with the rich brown background and Sancho's own skin colour, make the painting unusually warm in tone as well as feeling. Gainsborough has painted thinly over a reddish base with shading in a chocolate tone and minimal colder lights on Sancho's nose, chin and lips. The resulting face seems to glow and contrasts strongly with the vanishing effect so often suffered by the faces of black servants in the shadows of 18th-century portraits of their masters.

A 19th-century pamphlet describing Sancho's portrait cites a note on the back of the canvas in William Stevenson's hand inscribed 'This sketch by Mr. Gainsborough, of Bath, was done in one hour and forty minutes, November 29th, 1768.' It is likely that Sancho's portrait was indeed painted in November 1768, when the Duchess of Montagu was also sitting for her portrait at Bath. It is not known who paid for the portrait or indeed whether it may have been a gift from Gainsborough directly to Sancho. Although Sancho had ownership of it after he left service, it is possible that it was commissioned by the Duke or Duchess. (The Duke's father had, for example, a portrait of Daniel Eaton who had been his steward.)

Gainsborough and Sancho had plenty to discuss whilst the sitting for the portrait took place. They shared mutual friends such as Garrick, violin virtuoso Felice Giardini and, later, the preacher Dr Dodd. Both were convivial, keen amateur musicians, and prone to exceed 'the bounds of temperance' as Gainsborough's daughter Margaret expressed it (cited in Stainton, 1977, Introduction). It is possible that they knew each other before the sitting through the Montagus or Garrick.

As was appropriate for the portrait of a servant, the half-length painted oval format is modest and informal. Unlike lesser servants, however, Sancho is not wearing livery. He is dressed in a fashionable waistcoat with gold brocade edging and black necktie. He is shown without any attributes of his talents such as an instrument or a book, nor is he shown holding an object – so common a feature of poses of black slaves or servants in images where they are of secondary importance. Instead he is portrayed in the gentlemanly 'hand-in-waistcoat' pose, adopted by portraitists from etiquettes of posture. The hand-in-waistcoat pose signified the modest reserve of an English gentleman (Meyer, 1995, p. 60) and although the pose was ubiquitous it confirmed Sancho's image as a respectable Englishman.

One might expect an 18th-century African known for his literary talent to be portrayed with literary attributes and indeed the rather poor anonymous portrait of Francis Williams sets him in a library (Figure 2). As a result, the viewer immediately perceives a learned black man but perceives little of Williams's own character. Williams was educated at Cambridge, wrote poetry and set up a school in Jamaica. Williams's attendance on the governing council of Jamaica was blocked and throughout his life he suffered from assumptions that his learning was only of interest because he was black. Hume's uninformed comment that 'it is likely he is admired for slender accomplishments, like a parrot who speaks a few words plainly' is not undermined by a portrait which places the man within a poorly realised setting that contrives to be both exotic, with its lush landscape in the distance, and traditionally learned at the same time. In contrast, Sancho's portrait, with its relaxed but elegant and socially acceptable pose, allows Sancho's individuality to shine without distraction.

Gainsborough's portrait of Sancho is perhaps the most accomplished of British 18th-century portraits of black people. However, other portraits are significant because they provide us with an insight into black life which is quite different from the more common portrayals of black people in paintings as exotic accessories to the fashionable world, or in prints where they are depicted as ragged, amusing or socially dangerous caricatures inhabiting the margins or lowest ranks of society.

Despite Sancho's later life, it used to be believed that Sancho himself was depicted in this derogative way in Hogarth's Taste in High Life (Figure 3) and in a portrait of Lady Mary Churchill, Duchess of Montagu, with Charles, her page, attributed to Enoch Seeman (Figure 4). Taste in High Life was painted in 1742 as a satire on contemporary fashions and the print after it (Figure 3) was produced without Hogarth's permission (Paulson, 1989, p. 31). Hogarth's inclusion of the black boy is a rare visual criticism of the fashionable possession of slave boys as pets. Even in the 18th century the boy being petted condescendingly by his mistress was said to be Sancho. However, as Sancho's friend John Ireland stated in his work on Hogarth, Sancho would, in 1742, already have been significantly older than the little boy pictured.

Although Sancho was in service to Lady Mary Churchill, Duchess of Montagu, her portrait attributed to Seeman was probably painted in the 1720s and Sancho was not born until around 1729. Unusually, it is possible to identify the page boy as Charles 'ye Black of her Grace'. References to him in the family's cash books provide a few details to add to the picture. Like Sancho, he was fortunate in finding himself with the Montagu family for he was paid wages like an ordinary servant rather than a slave, and care was taken to ensure he was educated, nursed when he was ill and above all, well-clothed in fine livery or exotic outfits. He received an expensive 'black velvit cap' and his shoes were made by the Duchess's own shoemaker. Black people like Charles served in art and in life as exotic accessories reflecting the status, elegance and wealth of their owners. He wears livery (S. Llewellyn, Personal communication, 1996) and although he looks out of the canvas, he is clearly placed in a subservient position to the Duchess who is seated at a higher level and whose gaze rests far above his head.

This type of portrait with black retainers was well established by the 17th century and is illustrated by the typically exotic portrait of Louise de Kéroualle, Duchess of Portsmouth (Figure 5), in which the black page's dark skin is used to set off the fair complexion of the Duchess. In these images, the individuality of the boys is diminished by their role as signifiers of the other's social standing. It is their skin colour, their exotic clothing or their livery which matters because these items reflect their owner's status.

Artists generally shared this attitude. Thus, Dutch artist Hendrik Pothoven used detailed working drawings for pose, posture and clothes of the figures in his paintings but left the faces without detail because he would later paint them, more accurately, from life (R.J.A. te Rijdt, 1990, p. 367). However in the case of two exquisite drawings of the same black servant, Pothoven has drawn the face with considerable care (Figure 6). It has been suggested that it may have been unnecessary to paint the servant from life as in his case it was sufficient to work from the drawing (R.J.A. te Rijdt, 1990, p. 361). The figure is decorative and a good personal likeness was less important than for the other sitters. The drawings also illustrate the disturbing, confined beauty and exoticism often associated with slave children. The boy wears a dark metal slave collar with his livery, turban and pearl earring. Slaves' collars bore owners' details and confirmed property status.

Men as well as boys were reduced to stereotypical portrayal. Sancho's troublesome friend Julius Soubise was the favourite of the Duchess of Queensberry, becoming a riding and fencing assistant to Henry Angelo and later master of his own Academy in Bengal. Soubise was also infamous as a Don Juan and fop and became a symbol for extravagance and inappropriate pretension. 'A Mungo Macaroni' (Figure 7) was produced as one in a highly popular series of caricatures which used the figures of contemporary followers of fashion, the Macaronies, to satirise foolish aspirations. The print, published in 1772 by M. Darly, is probably a caricature of Soubise and his affectations. It has been further suggested that the intended victim of the caricature was Jeremiah Dyson, known as Mungo after the name had been given to him in a debate and who was thereafter frequently caricatured as a black man, in this case in the guise of Soubise (M. D. George, 1935, p. 82; G. Gerzina, 1995, p. 10). In the following year, 1773, Soubise's relationship with the Duchess of Queensberry, as well as his fondness for clothes, perfume and flowers, was mocked in a caricature of the pair fencing (Figure 8).

A more flattering representation of a black figure with a white companion occurs in the double portrait of Dido Elizabeth Belle with Lady Elizabeth Murray attributed to Johann Zoffany (Figure 9). Dido was born around 1763, the illegitimate daughter of Sir John Lindsay, nephew to Lord Mansfield. Lord Mansfield took Dido into his household at Kenwood, perhaps as a companion for his niece Elizabeth Murray, shown seated in the painting. Dido was treated with kindness and held a position balanced between family member and superior servant, joining the family and their guests for coffee, but not dinner (Adams, 1984, pp. 10–14). Dido steps forward whilst Elizabeth stops her reading to acknowledge Dido and reach towards her. Dido is wearing romantic garb of vague construction associated with masquerade dress. The specific features of Indian turban with an ostrich feather and diaphanous sash mark her costume as 'Eastern'. This costume is fancy dress for portraiture which foregrounds her ethnic origins ('Eastern' could apply to the West Indies in the rather vague notions of 18th-century exoticists). In addition, Dido points at the colour of her cheek. Elizabeth Murray wears a contemporary day dress in light fabrics which contrasts with the outmoded satin of Dido's outfit. However, satin continued to be worn at masquerades (A. Ribeiro, 1975, p. 241) and Dido's dress would therefore have been immediately acknowledged by the fashionable eye as a fancy costume. Contemporary and fancy costume were not usually combined in group portraits in this way: the painter evidently gave some thought to his treatment of Dido. He needed to display the affection between the two girls and the favour shown to Dido by Mansfield and Elizabeth, whilst retaining a decorous assertion of their different status. His choice of variant costume is a harmonious solution legible to 18th-century viewers who were familiar with black pages dressed in exotic clothing and turbans. Dido's air of activity in the picture further suggests her status – whilst Elizabeth could read at her leisure, Dido had duties to fulfil as a kind of superintendent over the dairy and poultry yard. As a product of the empire, Dido appropriately bears a plate of fruit suggesting the cornucopia of produce yielded up by the West and East Indies. This double portrait of Dido Belle and Elizabeth Murray is one of very few images of black women in the 18th century. It is particularly valuable for its representation of a respectable, identifiable black girl, rather than an anonymous attendant or the lewd or poor stereotypes which appeared in 18th- and 19th-century prints.

Like Dido Belle, Francis Barber benefited from a generous patron who treated him as an adopted child and bequeathed him a large inheritance. Barber was well known as Dr Johnson's servant, especially for the black social gatherings he held at Johnson's house. He was much beloved by Dr Johnson, for whom he worked almost continuously from 1752 to Johnson's death in 1784. Johnson took a strongly paternal interest in Barber's education and left his entire inheritance to him. One of the most famous images of a black figure today is an unfinished work, now in the Menil Foundation, executed by Reynolds around 1770 (N. Penny, 1986, pp. 245–6), frequently identified as Francis Barber (Figure 10).

The identification of the painting's subject as 'Frank' Barber probably stems from a confusion which arose in the 19th century between Frank Barber, Dr Johnson's servant, and Reynolds' own black servant (Reade, 1909, pp. 103–7). Sir George Beaumont, who bought the painting at auction in 1796, and had known Reynolds and probably his servant also, allowed it to be exhibited at the British Institution in 1813 as Sir Joshua Reynolds' black servant. But the work had become associated with Barber by 1857 and in 1861 the British Institution catalogue's confused misidentification read 'Barber, Frank, Servant of Sir Joshua Reynolds'.

It is known that Reynolds used his servant as a model. For example, he painted him as a young page holding the Marquess of Granby's horse in Granby's portrait in the Royal Collection (Northcote, 1819, p. 204). The Menil Foundation painting is heroic in mood but Reynolds appears in fact to have had a low opinion of his servant. When his servant was robbed, Reynolds was appalled to find the apprehended criminal under threat of execution and made his servant provide the convict with food from his own table (Northcote, 1819, p. 206). (Nor was this through any squeamishness about the death penalty for in 1788 Reynolds was publicly criticised for attending the execution of another servant personally known to him.) The painting by Reynolds is a study in painterly technique rather than a portrait as such and several versions after it result from his students being encouraged to copy it. The image embodies notions of the noble savage and is used to represent a type rather than an individual.

By contrast, another image once attributed to Reynolds but since relegated to 'English School' (E. Waterhouse, Personal communication to C. Blackie, 1961) certainly represents the portrait of an individual (Figure 11). He is usually identified as Olaudah Equiano, author of *The Interesting Narrative of the Life of Olaudah Equiano, or Gustavus Vassa, the African. Written by Himself*, first published in 1789. Equiano's early British slave narrative was an important weapon in the rallying movement against the slave trade. Born in Nigeria, Equiano was captured by slave-traders as a boy, served on a plantation in Virginia, in the Royal Navy during the Seven Years' War, and then acted as a trader for a Quaker owner before managing to buy his own freedom. Thereafter he joined the Phipps expedition to the Arctic seeking a Northeast Passage in 1773, acted as commissary for the Sierra Leone resettlement project, and toured all over England promoting the abolition of the slave trade. The identification of Equiano as the subject of the painting was originally made on the basis of a supposed similarity to the frontispiece engraving to *The Interesting Narrative* (Figure 12) (W. Fagg, Personal communication to J. Baker, 1961). It was quickly recognised that the painting could not be the original of the engraving by Daniel Orme after W. Denton as pose and costume are completely different. Nevertheless, the facial likeness was accepted despite the fact that Equiano's face in the frontispiece is long and narrow, especially in the lower half of the face, contrasting with the jowly figure in the painting. Christopher Fyfe raised doubts about their likeness in a verbal address in 1994 but the identification of the portrait as Equiano has generally continued. However, the date of the painting presents a further obstacle to identification of the sitter as Equiano. Judging by the costume and style, the portrait is unlikely to have been painted after 1765. Yet from the time of his kidnap until 1762, Equiano spent most of his time working at sea and from 1762 to 1766 he was in the West Indies. From 1767 to 1773 Equiano was based in London but was actively working on commercial vessels sailing to the Mediterranean and the West Indies (Carretta, 1995, p. ix). It seems unlikely that Equiano would have had the opportunity to have his portrait painted before 1767 or that he would have found time in later years and not mentioned the event in his narrative.

Although this portrait may not be of Equiano, it bears mute testimony to the presence in Britain of black individuals who were of sufficient status to have their portraits painted even if we do not know who they are today. (Fyfe has suggested that the portrait is of another author of a slave narrative, Ottobah Cugoano (Fyfe, 1994). However, Cugoano was enslaved around 1770 and the probable date of the portrait therefore discounts him also.) Whoever it is, the portrait is a fine one. It possesses that disturbing forthrightness and presence which Equiano himself noticed the first time he saw a portrait in 1756. Despite the novelty of Western images, Equiano immediately understood the function of portraits, although he added a layer of superstition to his recognition of their intention:

> and when I immediately after observed a picture hanging in the room, which appeared constantly to look at me, I was still more affrighted, having never seen such things as these before. At one time I thought it was something relative to magic; and not seeing it move, I thought it might be some way the whites had to keep their great men when they died'

> (Carretta, 1995, p. 63).

A few portraits keep alive the memory of 18th-century black people also. They hint at the far-reaching consequences of Britain's commercial empire with its transatlantic traffic in people, goods, ideas and culture.

Trade with both the Indies involved Britain herself in cultural change as the peoples and cultures of those exotic worlds came to her ports. Sancho and the other black people whose faces have been recorded for us in portraits were unusually fortunate. Yet Sancho embodies many of the ambiguities and strengths of the black experience in Britain. Born on the Atlantic between Africa and the West Indies he found the means to free himself by turning to the Montagu family for patronage and appealing to their sense of his intelligence and promise. Many slaves simply ran away to the anonymous crowds of the city. Although Sancho was keenly aware of the horrors of slavery, his urban society was dominated by its products. He could not avoid these and he traded in sugar. Deflecting racism, Sancho claimed an equal right to independence, to partake in and contribute to English culture, to become a connoisseur and a man of letters. Sancho's humour, irony, literary expression and cultured zest for life somehow reconciled the differences. The man represented in Sancho's letters and in Gainsborough's portrait was confident in his own abilities and took an ironic view of his own life because he recognised the madness of his surrounding culture and the position it assigned to black people. The suggestion of a laugh or a wry comment playing on his lips in Gainsborough's portrait thus aptly captured Sancho's character and his understanding of his own position in 18th-century London as an African man of letters.

Acknowledgements

I am indebted to His Grace, the Duke of Buccleuch and Queensberry for access to Boughton House and its Archive and to Tessa Murdoch and Gareth Fitzpatrick who drew my attention to the presence of references to Sancho and Charles in the Montagu family's account books. I am deeply grateful to John Ralph Willis for making available his collection of Sancho's letters.

I have received valuable assistance and advice from Jacob Simon, Lucy Clark, Kathleen Soriano and the staff of the Heinz Archive at the National Portrait Gallery; Nicholas Penny, Judy Egerton and Elspeth Hector at the National Gallery; Andrew Wilde of Thos. Agnew & Sons Ltd., Sacha Llewellyn and Varvara Shavrova. Hugh Belsey, Polly Rewt and Sukhdev Sandhu have generously shared both scholarship and enthusiasm.

Bibliography

Primary sources:

Boughton House Archive:
Boughton House Cash Books 1727–1737.
Inventory of Paintings in Boughton House, 1832 (BH10);
Lady Cardigan Account from 7 July 1749 to 10 July 1755;
The Dutchess of Montagu's Account from 17 July 1769 to 22 July 177–.

Northamptonshire County Record Office:
George Cardigan's Account Books, 1755–1772 (NCRO X4573).

Collection of John Ralph Willis:
Letters from Ignatius Sancho to William Stevenson;
Letters from or on behalf of Elizabeth Sancho mostly to William Stevenson;
Letters from William Sancho to William Stevenson.

British Library Department of Manuscripts:
Letter from George Cumberland to Richard Dennison Cumberland (BM Add Mss., 36, 514, f. 29);
Letter from George Cumberland to Richard Dennison Cumberland (BM Add Mss., 36, 492, f. 204).

Greenwich Local History Society, Woodlands Local History Library:
Notes prepared by Neil Rhind on Montague House as part of forthcoming publication on Blackheath Village.

Secondary sources:

Adams, G. (1984), 'Dido Elizabeth Belle: A Black Girl at Kenwood', *Camden History Review*;

Alister, C. (1978), 'Montague House, Blackheath and "The Delicate Investigation"', in *Transactions of the Greenwich and Lewisham Antiquarian Society*, vol. 8, no. 6, pp. 234–46;

Angelo, H. (1828–1830), *Reminiscences of Henry Angelo, with Memoirs of His Life, Father and Friends*, 2 vols, London: Henry Colburn;

Armstrong, W. (1904), *Gainsborough and his Place in English Art*, p. 278, London: William Heinemann;

Boggs, J. S. (1971), *The National Gallery of Canada*, London: Thames and Hudson;

Brilliant, R. (1991), *Portraiture*, London: Reaktion Books; Cambridge: Harvard University Press;

Bryant, J. (1990), *The Iveagh Bequest: Kenwood*, London: London Historic House Museums Trust;

Bush, J. (1993), 'Moving on – and looking back', *History Workshop*, Issue 36;

Clarkson, T. (1836), *The History of the Rise, Progress and Accomplishment of the Abolition of the Slave Trade, by the British Parliament*, 3 vols, London: Longman & Co;

Cormack, M. (1991), *The Paintings of Thomas Gainsborough*, Cambridge: Cambridge University Press;

Cunnington, P. (1974), *Costume of Household Servants; from the Middle Ages to 1900*, London: A and C Black;

Dabydeen, D. (1985), *Hogarth's Blacks: Images of blacks in eighteenth century English art*, Kingston-upon-Thames: Dangaroo Press;

Donald, D. (1996), *The Age of Caricature. Satirical prints in the reign of George III*, New Haven and London: Published for the Paul Mellon Centre for Studies in British Art by Yale University Press;

Edwards, P. (1992), 'Unreconciled Strivings and Ironic Strategies: Three Afro-British Authors of the Georgian Era, Ignatius Sancho, Olaudah Equiano, Robert Wedderburn', *Occasional Papers* no. 34, Edinburgh: Centre of African Studies, Edinburgh University;

Edwards, P. and D. Dabydeen (1991, 1995), *Black Writers in Britain 1760–1890*, Edinburgh: Edinburgh University Press;

Edwards, P. and J. Walvin (eds) (1983), *Black Personalities in the Era of the Slave Trade*, London: Macmillian;

Equiano, O. (1995), *The Interesting Narrative and other writings*, ed. V. Carretta, New York and London: Penguin Books;

Fryer, P. (1984), *Staying Power. The History of Black People in Britain*; London: Pluto Press;

Fryer, P. (1993), *Aspects of British Black History*, London: Index Books;

Fulcher, G. W. (1856), *Life of Thomas Gainsborough*, R.A., London: Longman, Brown, Green and Longman;

Fyfe, C. (1994), *To remind us of Paul*, delivered as a tribute at a conference in honour of Paul Edwards, Edinburgh;

George, M. D. (1935), *Catalogue of political and personal satires: preserved in the Department of Prints and Drawings in the British Museum*, vol. 5, 1771–1783, London: British Museum;

George, M. D. (1951), *London Life in the Eighteenth century*, London: London School of Economics and Political Science;

George, M. D. (1967), *Hogarth to Cruikshank: social change in graphic satire*, London: Allen Lane, The Penguin Press;

Gerzina, G. (1995), *Black England: Life before Emancipation*, London: John Murray;

Graves, A. and W. V. Cronin (1899–1901), *A History of the Works of Sir Joshua Reynolds, P.R.A*, 4 vols, London: H. Graves & Co.;

Hecht, J. J. (1954), 'Continental and Colonial Servants in Eighteenth-Century England', *The Smith College Studies in History*, no. 40;

Hecht, J. J. (1956), *The Domestic Servant Class in Eighteenth-Century England*, London: Routledge and Kegan Paul;

Honour, H. (1989), *The Image of the Black in Western Art. IV. From the American Revolution to World War I*, Cambridge and London: copyright by Menil Foundation Inc., Houston, distributed by Harvard University Press;

Hubbard, R. H. (1957), *The National Gallery Catalogue of Paintings and Sculpture*, vol. 1, Older Schools, Ottawa and Toronto: University of Toronto Press;

Ireland, J. (1791–1798), *Hogarth illustrated from his own manuscripts*, 3 vols, London: J. E. J. Boydell;

Kaplan, S. and E. Nogrady Kaplan (1989), *The Black Presence in the Era of the American Revolution*, Amherst: University of Massachusetts Press;

Kapp, H. (1972), *Daniel Gardner 1750–1805*, London: Greater London Council;

Laskin, M. Jr. and M. Pantazzi (eds) (1987), *Catalogue of the National Gallery of Canada, Ottawa, European Painting, Sculpture and Decorative Arts*, vol. 1, Ottawa: National Gallery of Canada/National Museums of Canada;

Locke, A. (ed.) (1940), *The Negro in Art: a pictorial record of the negro artist and of the negro theme in art*, Washington: Associates in Negro Folk Education;

Lumsden, I. G. (1991), *Gainsborough in Canada*, Fredericton, New Brunswick: Beaverbrook Art Gallery;

Meyer, A. (1995), 'Re-dressing classical statuary: the eighteenth-century "hand-in-waistcoat" portrait', in *The Art Bulletin*, vol. 77, no. 1 (March);

The Monthly Review; or Literary Journal: (January–December, 1783), vol. 69, pp. 492–7, London: R. Griffiths;

Murdoch, T. (ed.) (1992), *Boughton House: The English Versailles*, (especially Appendix 1: 'The Portraits' by Malcolm Rogers), London: Faber and Faber/Christie's;

Nichols, J. and G. Steevens (1808–1817), *The Genuine Works of William Hogarth*, 3 vols, London: Longman;

Northcote, J. (1819), *The Life of Sir Joshua Reynolds*, vol. I, London: Printed for Henry Colburn, Conduit Street;

Ogude, S. E. (1983), *Genius in bondage, a study of the origins of African literature in English*, Ife-Ife;

Paulson, R. (1971), *Hogarth: His Life, Art, and Times*, 2 vols, New Haven and London: Yale University Press;

Paulson, R. (1989), *Hogarth's Graphic Works*, London: The Print Room;

Paulson, R. (1991/1992/1993), *Hogarth*, 3 vols, New Brunswick and London, 1991, New Brunswick, New Jersey, 1992, Cambridge, 1993;

Penny, N. (ed.) (1986), *Reynolds*, London: Royal Academy of Arts catalogue in association with Weidenfeld and Nicholson;

Pointon, M. (1993), *Hanging the Head: Portraiture and social formation in eighteenth-century England*, New Haven and London: published for The Paul Mellon Centre for Studies in British Art by Yale University Press;

Reade, A. L. (1912), *Johnsonian Gleanings, Part II: Francis Barber, The Doctor's Negro Servant*, London: Arden Press;

Ribeiro, A. (1984), *The Dress Worn at Masquerades in England, 1730 to 1790, and its relation to fancy dress in portraiture*, New York and London: Garland;

Riely, J. (1983), 'Henry William Bunbury: the amateur as caricaturist', in *Henry William Bunbury 1750–1811*, Sudbury: Gainsborough's House Society;

te Rijdt, R. J. A. (1990), 'Figuurstudies door Hendrik Pothoven en enkele biografische gevevens', *Leids Kunsthistorisch Jaarboek*, 8, pp. 345–58;

Sancho, I. (1782), *Letters of the late Ignatius Sancho, an African, To which are Prefixed, Memoirs of his Life* first ed., 2 vols, London: J. Nichols;

Sancho, I. (1803), *Letters of the late Ignatius Sancho, an African, to which are Prefixed Memoirs of his Life by Joseph Jekyll, Esq, MP* fifth ed., London: Printed for William Sancho;

Sancho, I. (1968), with a new introduction by Paul Edwards, *Letters of the Late Ignatius Sancho: An African to which are Prefixed Memoirs of His Life by Joseph Jekyll, Esq, MP*, facsimile reprint of fifth edition, London: Dawsons of Pall Mall, The Colonial History Series;

Sancho, I. (1994), Edwards, P. and P. Rewt (eds) (1994), *The Letters of Ignatius Sancho*, Edinburgh: Edinburgh University Press;

Sandiford, K. A. (1988), *Measuring the Moment: Strategies of Protest in Eighteenth-Century Afro-English Writing*, London and Toronto: Associated University Presses;

Shyllon, F. O. (1974), *Black Slaves in Britain*, Oxford: Oxford University Press for Institute of Race Relations;

Shyllon, F. O. (1977), *Black People in Britain*, London: Oxford University Press for Institute of Race Relations;

Smith, J. T. (1828), *Nollekens and his Times*, London: Henry Colburn;

Stainton, L. (1977), *Gainsborough and his Musical Friends*, London: Greater London Council

Sunderland, J. (1986), 'J. H. Mortimer', in *Walpole Society*, vol. 52;

Sypher, W. (1942), *Guinea's Captive Kings: British Anti-Slavery Literature of the XVIIIth Century*, Chapel Hill: The University of North Carolina Press;

Tibbles, A. (ed.) (1995), *Transatlantic Slavery. Against Human Dignity*, London: HMSO for National Museums and Galleries on Merseyside;

Wake, J. (1954), *The Brudenells of Deene*, London: Cassell and Company Ltd.;

Walvin, J. (1971), *The Black Presence: A Documentary History of the Negro in England*, London: Orbach and Chambers;

Walvin, J. (1986), *England, Slaves and Freedom 1776–1838*, Basingstoke: Macmillan;

Walvin, J. (1993), *Black Ivory: A History of British Slavery*, London: Fontana Press;

Waterhouse, E. (1958), *Gainsborough*, London: Edward Hulton;

Wendorf, R. (ed.) (1983), *Articulate Images: The Sister Arts from Hogarth to Tennyson*, Minneapolis: University of Minnesota Press;

Whitley, W. T. (1915), *Thomas Gainsborough*, London: Smith, Elder & Co.;

Williamson, G. C. (1921), *Daniel Gardner*, London and New York: Bodley Head;

Willis, J. R. (1980), 'New Light on the Life of Ignatius Sancho: Some Unpublished Letters', *Slavery & Abolition*, vol. 1, no. 3, December;

Woodall, M. (ed.) (1963), *The Letters of Thomas Gainsborough*, Ipswich: The Cupid Press;

Wright, J. (1979), 'Ignatius Sancho (1729–1780), African Composer in England', *Black Perspective in Music*, vol. 7, no. 2, Fall;

Wright, J. (1981), *Works, Ignatius Sancho (1729-1780), An Early African Composer in England: the Collected Edition of his Music in Facsimile*, New York and London: Garland;

Wright, J. (1986), Lotz, R. and I. Pegg (eds) (1986), 'Early African Musicians in Britain', in *Under the Imperial carpet. Essays in black history 1780–1950*, Crawley: Rabbit Press;

Young, M. J. (1806), *Memoirs of Mrs. Crouch*, London: J. Asperne.

Chapter 2

Ignatius Sancho: An African Man of Letters

Sukhdev Sandhu

> *Sale of a Negro Boy.* – In the account of the trial of
> John Rice, who was hanged for forgery at Tyburn, May
> 4, 1763, it is said, 'A commision of bankruptcy having
> been taken out against Rice, his effects were sold by
> auction, and among the rest his negro boy.' I could not
> have believed such a thing could have taken place so
> lately; there is little doubt it was the last of the kind
>
> (Letter from A.A to *Notes and Queries*, 1858).

A.A. was wrong. In the years following his letter of baffled
disgust to *Notes and Queries*, many of the antiquarians,
genealogists and men of letters who made up the readership
of that journal, wrote in to provide subsequent examples of
African men and women being parcelled off to the highest
bidder at public auctions held in the centre of the English
capital. A.A.'s question, the ensuing lost-and-found
advertisements, and the details of slave auctions which
were reprinted in *Notes and Queries*, point to the speed
and ease with which London's malodorous past had been
forgotten even in some of the most learned quarters within
English society. Although slavery had been finally abolished
in the West Indies barely twenty years before, it required
archivists and antiquarians to fill in the large chinks that
were already emerging in the public memory.

The black presence in England did not, as is popularly
imagined, begin with the arrival of the 492 Jamaican
passengers (and eight stowaways) on the *Empire Windrush*
at Tilbury in 1948. Evidence of black people at work and
play during the 18th century is not confined to the realm of
the visual arts; blacks are also commonly to be found fleet-
footing their ways through the metropolitan literature of
that period. In Thomas Brown's *Amusements Serious and
Comical* (1702) the narrator is accompanied on his ambles
through the byways and slyways of the capital by a
quizzical Indian. One of the first people they see is another
'sooty Dog' who 'could do nothing but Grin, and shew his
Teeth, and cry, Coffee, Sir, Tea, will you please to walk in,

Sir, a fresh Pot upon my word.' (Brown, 1702, p. 27).

Over the following decades an increasing number of black people were brought over to London as servants by planters, naval officers and Government officials returning from the Caribbean. So many arrived that it comes as no surprise that when, nearly a century after Thomas Brown's comic rambles through the metropolis, William Wordsworth sat down to compose the 'Residence in London' section of his autobiographical poem, *The Prelude*, he recalled the exotic cosmopolitanism he had found thronging the streets of the capital after the three years of blanched provincialism spent at Cambridge:

> Now homeward through the thickening hubbub...
> The Hunter-indian; Moors,
> Malays, Lascars, the Tartar, the Chinese,
> And Negro Ladies in white muslin Gowns

(Wordsworth, [1850] 1985, p. 143).

African characters were also commonly found on the London stage. Thomas Southerne's adaptation of Aphra Behn's *Oroonoko* (1696) was extremely popular and was performed at least once a season throughout the century until 1808. The type of black most often portrayed was the noble savage: eloquent, regal in appearance and birthright, he inevitably ended the play committing suicide rather than be taken into captivity. His language was Latinate, his demeanour dignified, his character entirely humourless. Only in the final three decades of the century did a more vibrant form of characterisation emerge – that of the comic negro. This stock character – often named Mungo, Marianne or Sambo – was a ridiculous but usually affectionate version of those black servants so commonly found in 18th-century aristocratic households. In Isaac Bickerstaffe's *Love In The City* (1767) and *The Padlock* (1768) the blacks are portrayed as earthy and good-natured. They speak in mongrel idioms very different from the high-flown grandiloquence of *Oroonoko* or *Inkle and Yarico*.

As the abolitionist movement began to flourish in the 1770s and 1780s, it became almost impossible to avoid the constant flow of anti-slavery poems, tracts and broadsides issuing forth from the printing presses. While of importance to historians, very little of this material possesses literary merit. The negro became a sentimental trope: he was usually shown as helpless, abased, solely reliant on the Christian goodwill of the European to rescue him from his miserable plight. He was rarely given dialogue to speak, the individual details of his abduction and transportation were omitted. Such texts completely lack grit and bite.

The first book by an African to be published in England was *A Narrative of the Most Remarkable Particulars in the Life of James Albert Ukawsaw Gronniosaw, An African Prince, Written by Himself* (1772). Dictated to 'a young Lady of the town of Leominster', it tells of the author's capture in Borno, Nigeria, and his subsequent travails in the Americas, Holland and England. Crammed with religious interjections and parables of dubious value, Gronniosaw's is an interesting start to the history of black British literature, but one that is rather didactic and over-determined by the Quaker beliefs of both the author and its intended audience.

Other black texts to emerge in the final decades of the century include Ottobah Cugoano's *Thoughts and Sentiments on the Evil and Wicked Traffic of the Slavery and Commerce of the Human Species* (1787), and a report of a speech attacking the slave trade delivered in London during 1791 by Prince Naimbanna of Sierra Leone. Most celebrated is *The Interesting Narrative of the Life of Olaudah Equiano, Or Gustavus Vassa, The African. Written by Himself* (1789). It went through nine editions in five years and sold thousands of copies as a result of the author's extensive reading tours throughout the United Kingdom. The book is in equal parts ethnographic treatise, travel narrative, spiritual autobiography and, perhaps most importantly, abolitionist polemic. Before he died in 1797, Equiano spent the last decade of his life firing off missives to metropolitan newspapers, helping with schemes to resettle the capital's black poor in Sierra Leone and, in effect, serving as the first black politician in England.

Sancho's name has come down to us through the centuries chiefly on account of his friendship with the writer, Laurence Sterne. As well as being a country pastor, Sterne was the author of *Tristram Shandy*, one of the most celebrated novels of the 18th century. Published in five parts between 1759 and 1767, it consists of nine volumes and well over 500 pages. It is narrated by the eponymous Tristram who tries to tell the story of his life from conception to adulthood. But, in a parody of the sequential, linear plots of many novels written during the century, the narrator's attempts to provide a lucid account of his life are constantly interrupted by digressions on topics such as the importance of knots or long noses. The tale is studded with lists and inventories of diseases, philosophers and even literary devices. Marbled pages, blank spaces, various squiggles and illustrative diagrams break up the flow of words. Even normal grammar is eschewed with dashes replacing full stops to lend the novel even more of a hustling, dizzying quality.

However, it was a passage in Sterne's sermon, 'Job's Account of the Shortness and Troubles of Life' (1760) about 'how bitter a draught' slavery was, that initially inspired Sancho to write to the celebrated author. Why not, he asked, 'give one half-hour's attention to slavery, as it is this day practised in our West Indies. – That subject, handled in your striking manner, would ease the yoke (perhaps) of many – but if only of one – Gracious God! – what a feast to a benevolent heart!' (Edwards and Rewt, 1994, p. 86).

Sterne – whose own father had died of a fever in 1731 after his regiment had been sent by the Duke of Newcastle to Jamaica to put down a slave uprising – was understandably delighted to receive this letter. Most black people in England were negligibly educated. They certainly did not read the work of learned authors such as Sterne. In his reply to Sancho, he promised to weave a tale 'of the sorrows of a friendless poor negro-girl' into his narrative (Curtis, 1935, p. 286). The ninth, and final, book of *Shandy* also included an argument for the humanity of negroes that earned Sterne posthumous acclaim from English and French abolitionists.

Sancho's published letters reveal a heavy stylistic debt to Sterne. His use of dashes as the chief form of punctuation rather than stops or commas has the effect of hobbling the reader. These dashes look like splinters strewn across the page. It is not always easy to glean immediately the sense of many of the passages: we are forced to pay particular scrutiny to each fragment of prose that is squeezed between the dashes. Instead of hurtling through each letter, each narrative, we are constantly forced to slow down, to accustom ourselves to this very individual authorial voice.

There are a number of reasons why Sancho, who was both widely and deeply read in the classic works of English literature, should feel compelled to adapt Sterne's style for his own letters. One is that he identified closely with many of the characters and their mishaps in *Tristram Shandy*.

Almost all of the characters in Sterne's novel are ravaged by illness. Tristram's father has sciatica; Tristram himself is asthmatic and had the bridge of his nose permanently damaged by the improper use of forceps by the midwife. Indeed, Tristram's nose was as flat as that of Sancho. Like Uncle Toby, and like Sterne himself whose bout of tuberculosis damaged his vocal chords and left him with a weak, cracked voice, Sancho had some problems when it came to talking. His biographer, Jekyll, tells us that he had an ambition to perform on the stage but 'a defective and incorrigible articulation rendered it abortive' (Edwards and Rewt, 1994, p. 23). It was ill-health that cut short

Sancho's service with the Montagu family and led him to open his grocery. As the years passed he was increasingly wracked by gout, dropsy, corpulency and asthma. Yet, just as the characters in Sterne's novel maintain their humour and their defiance despite their ailments, Sancho's letters rarely show him succumbing to self-pity or defeatism.

One of the key themes of Sterne's novel is that of naming. Tristram's father believes that particular names determine the behaviour, conduct and the success that individuals may achieve during their lives. He had gone to the length of writing a dissertation on the fact that, in his expert opinion, Tristram was the very worst name imaginable. He intends to call his son Trismegistus and is mortified when he learns that his servant, Susannah, had garbled the child's name to the vicar at the baptising ceremony. Sancho, like many of his fellow blacks in England at this time, owed his name to the mixture of contempt and condescension with which many aristocrats viewed slaves. The Greenwich sisters gave Sancho his surname on a whim, on the strength of a comic resemblance to a fictional character. They could do this because no one believed blacks would – or *could* – ever attain such status in society that their names would come to embarrass them. But, through the patronage of successive members of the Montagu family and his own intellectual graft, Sancho evaded the fate that the slave trade and the condescension of the sisters had intended for him. Like Tristram, Sancho exhibits such fortitude and warm humanity as to discredit any theory that would claim an individual's life trajectory is determined from the time he or she is named.

However, the main reason for Sancho's emulation of Sterne's style is not merely aesthetic, but because he believes the dashes, digressions and textual games serve a deeply moral purpose. In his sermon, 'Philanthropy Recommended' (1760), Sterne recounts the parable of the Good Samaritan, who, unlike the wealthier travellers who had preceded him on that route, had been prepared to turn his attention and compassion towards the stricken victim lying by the roadside. Discussing his own narrative methods in the first volume of *Tristram Shandy*, he draws a parallel with historiographers who might consider writing their books in a straightforward, sequential style. Such a technique is plausible, Sterne argues, but 'morally speaking, impossible' (Sterne, [1759] 1983, p. 32).

Linearity, we learn, is tantamount to selfishness. We must be prepared always to look around us, be prepared to halt, to be diverted by what is going on in the corners, the crevices, the byways of life. These side routes are full of value, pleasure and goodness. This amounts to a doctrine which urges us to be concerned for the defective, the maimed, those who are unable to hasten along the straight paths of economic or social success. It is hardly surprising that Sancho, who often found difficulty in feeding and clothing his family, and who required a gift of old quills in order even to be able to write, should praise Sterne for being 'truly a noble philanthropist' in his work.

By using dashes to break up his prose, Sancho also sought to ironise 18th-century racial theorists such as Edward Long and Samuel Estwick who equated linearity with the ability both to think straight and to be capable of rational thought. Africans, they argued, could not deal with linearity. Therefore blacks were not truly human and enslaving them was neither immoral nor against nature. So common was the stress on linearity in anti-abolitionist literature that William Dickson decided to mount a counter-attack in *Letters on Slavery* (1789):

> The streets of many towns in this kingdom, and even of this metropolis, are crooked. If our ancestors, who laid out those streets were to be half as much calumniated as the negroes have been, it would probably be asserted, that they could not draw a straight line, between two given points, in the same plane (p. 82).

One has always to remember that Sancho's life lacked

fluidity, causality, organic progression. From the time he was born aboard a slave ship he had suffered discontinuity, upheaval, at best only a stuttering momentum. His parents could hardly have expected that they themselves would be sold into captivity and that their child would be born into bondage. Nor could it have been anticipated that he would somehow elude a short, brutish life toiling under the Caribbean sun by being shipped to Greenwich. How many imported slaves had the good fortune to attract mentors in the form of the 2nd Duke of Montagu? Or to end their lives circulating amongst actors, writers and art connoisseurs while owning their own business a stone's throw away from the Houses of Parliament? Looked at in the context of the poverty and the continual disruptions he faced throughout his life, Sancho's responsiveness towards Sterne's writings, which advocated Samaritanism, practical virtue, and good humour as aids towards a good life, appears all too understandable.

Sancho's studious creolisation of Sterne's aesthetic should remind us forcibly that he was a man of letters. For all the skill and canniness with which Equiano imbued his polemical memoirs, he still used prose instrumentally, tactically, in a manner that is largely absent from Sancho's *Letters*. This is not a criticism for Equiano was writing in 1789, at the height of abolitionist fervour, and his book was specifically intended to contribute to the Anti-Slavery Society campaign.

Sancho, in contrast, wrote his letters, at least initially, with little regard for publication. For him, writing was a way of temporarily escaping the routines and stresses of running a grocery. This does not mean that his letters were not crammed with details of his daily retailing existence. They were. But, at the same time, Sancho toyed, he frolicked with metaphors and words to such an extent that we feel that it is only in these letters to his friends that he could fully give vent to his imagination. He himself was aware of this and ended one note, 'Is not that – *a good one?*'

Humour is perhaps the dominant tone of these letters. Sancho loved to create comic neologisms: he described a friend, John Ireland, as an 'eccentric phizpoop'; elsewhere he exclaimed 'alas! an unlucky parciplepliviaplemontis seizes my imagination'. At one level, these examples show the influence of Sterne – another inveterate coiner of words – on Sancho's writing. But, as well as impress upon his readers his facility with the English language, something his comparative vocal difficulties prevented him from doing upon the stage, one senses that Sancho wants to replenish the stocks of the national language. One could see this as a lexical version of the many acts of charity which he undertook in the metropolis on behalf of strangers and friends alike. Perhaps it is also a case of the ex-slave wanting to shake off any vestiges of social and intellectual passivity, and, instead, to be a creator, a free manufacturer of words and concepts.

Sancho's playful approach was confined not just to language, but to the very grammar and appearance of his letters. In a note to John Meheux, First Clerk in the Board of Control, he wrote:

> I hope confound the ink! – what a blot! Now don't you dare suppose I was in fault – No Sir, the pen was diabled – the paper worse, – there was a concatenation of ill-sorted chances – all – all – coincided to contribute to that fatal blot – which has so disarranged my ideas, that I must perforce finish before I had half disburthened my head and heart.

At this point, the first edition reproduces the author's original black blot.

Sancho is sometimes erroneously thought of as a rather stuffy, pompous writer. Much of his humour is actually rather lewd and earthy. In one letter he provides a gruesomely vivid description of a journey he had made with his friend, William Stevenson, on a sweaty, cramped and ill-tempered stage coach. The driver tried to palm

Sancho off with 'a bad shilling', cursing him when he pointed this out. Sancho's breathing space was further restricted by the arrival of an obese couple:

> after keeping us half an hour in sweet converse of the – of the *blasting* kind – how that fat woman waxed wrath with her plump master, for his being serene –... how he ventured his head out of the coach-door, and swore liberally – whilst his ——, in direct line with poor Stevenson's nose, entertained him with *sound* and sweetest of exhalations.

There was further misery to come. Before the journey was over Stevenson had been sick and the fat couple's child had pissed on his legs.

Sancho was not averse to a dash of sauciness. '[W]hat books have you read?' he asked John Meheux, '– what lasses gallanted?'; he mocked Stevenson for sending him a gloomy letter, 'thou hast only one mouth to feed – one back to clothe – and one wicked member to indulge'. Such passages remind us that Sancho was reputed to have spent much of the 1750s living a life of excess and dissipation in the metropolis.

Yet the shadow of illness, poverty and bereavement is never too far away from Sancho's correspondence. Perhaps it was only through a certain ebullience and forced jocularity that he could hope to fend off gloomier thoughts. Much of this humour was self-reflexive: 'The gout seized me yesterday morning...I looked rather black all day.'

Such remarks should not be taken as examples of self-loathing or of a pitiable eagerness to amuse his correspondents. In a letter to John Meheux, he observed that his pen

> sucks up more liquor than it can carry, and so of course disgorges it at random. – I will that ye observe the above simile to be a good one – not the cleanliest in nature, I own – but as pat to the purpose as

> dram-drinking to a bawd – or oaths to a sergeant of the
> guards – or – or – dullness to a Black-a-moor – Good –
> excessive good!

It is a passage worthy of some attention. At one level, it
demonstrates amply Sancho's love of literary play. The tone
is sly, ironic, mock-heroic; it is as far removed from the
strait-laced polemic of other black writers during this
period – Ottobah Cugoano and Naimbanna for example –
as can be imagined.

The second half of the sentence, however, dispels any
fancy we might have that Sancho was apolitical or, as
Norma Meyers has alleged, a Sambo figure. As with Sterne,
the teasing and joking in this letter had a strong moral
underpinning. Sancho rarely indulged in writing for
writing's sake. After his allusions to the alcohol-guzzling
prostitute and the foul-mouthed sergeant, Sancho was keen
to show himself as stuttering, desperately g(r)asping for a
third analogy to give balance to the sentence. The dashes,
the repetition of 'or' show that time was running out. He
would cleave to a simile, any simile, that would shore up
this sentence in which he found himself drowning. Which
cliché did he resort to? That of blacks being stupid. Sancho
was well aware of how common such beliefs were and
frequently challenged them in his letters. Here the clear
implication is that such noxious utterances can only stem
from writers seeking to lend their prose a sheen, a
rhetorical (both in its literal and pejorative sense) sonority.
It is a subtle and witty demolition of racist discourse, as
befitted a man of Sancho's learning and eloquence.

Having led such a vagarious and unpredictable life,
Sancho was understandably keen to dispense the benefits of
his accumulated wisdom. The many years he had spent as a
senior servant in the Montagu household gave him a degree
of confidence and convincing gravitas when it came to
imparting advice to his correspondents. His conversion 'for
my sins' to Methodism in 1769 encouraged him to believe
in the moral, reformatory role of literature. What is more,

his letter-writing itself can be regarded as a means of charting and plotting the trajectory of his life in order to discern its providential structure more clearly. Given the enforced dislocation and peripateia for millions of Africans during the 18th century, the need for some vertebration – both literary and theological – became highly important. In letters to two black friends, Julius Soubise and Charles Lincoln, Sancho detailed the importance of ignoring the derision and 'frothy gibes' of others in order to write and read sensibly: 'note down the occurrences of every day – to which add your own observation of men and things – The more you habituate yourself to minute investigation, the stronger you will make your mind – ever taking along with you in all your researches the word of God'.

It is clear that many of Sancho's correspondents enjoyed being hectored and chided by him. He told his friend Lydia Leach that 'for writing conversable letters you are wholly unfit – no talent – no nature – no style – stiff – formal – and unintelligible'. The tone is mock furious – Sancho gums rather than bites his epistolatory 'victim'. Nevertheless he was often anxious that his constant imparting of advice might appear presumptuous and over-intrusive. He constantly peppered his letters with apologies for becoming too pietistic: 'thou smilest at my futile notions – Why preach to thee?'; 'I have done preaching. – Old folks love to seem wise.' One may debate the extent to which these statements express genuine contrition. Even so, in his wariness of preaching we may detect a certain timidity about overstepping the thresholds of politeness and decorum. In a letter to Jack Wingrave, Sancho defended the honour and morality of Indian natives before going on to denounce the 'uniformly wicked' conduct of the English in their colonies abroad. He stops abruptly: 'But enough – it is a subject that sours my blood – and I am sure will not please the friendly bent of your social affections.'

In comparison to other black writers such as Equiano and Cugoano, some have felt that Sancho's style is too florid and overwrought. There is certainly some truth in this charge. Sancho, in common with many senior servants who had worked in aristocratic households during the 18th century, was keen to appear cultured and genteel. Both this and his belief in the importance of self-improvement account for the occasional stuffiness of tone in the letters. At the same time, one can exaggerate the extent of Sancho's orotundity. It is worth emphasising how often he used metaphors involving everyday foodstuffs and domestic items with which to lard his prose: 'man is an absurd animal –...friendship without reason – hate without reflection – knowledge (like Ashley's punch in small quantities) without judgment'. In one of his many excursions into literary criticism, Sancho regretted the commonplace insipidity of much of Voltaire's *Semiramis*, but adds 'from dress – scenery – action – and the rest of playhouse garniture – it may show well and go down – like insipid fish with good sauce'. It is particularly ironic that Sancho criticised Voltaire since his son, Billy, went on to become the first black publisher in the Western world, and issued, among other titles, that author's *La Henriade*.

Standing at the shop counter every day, gossiping, joking, often griping about his ailing profits with customers for hours on end, Sancho's vocation supplied him with a ready stock of gags. Some are excruciating. He recounted one exasperating conversation with a customer thus: 'what? – what! – Dates! Dates! – Am not I a grocer? – pun the second.' On another occasion, Sancho made satiric use of the tea that he sold in his shop. Enthusing about the poetry of the black American, Phillis Wheatley, he wished 'that every member of each house of parliament had one of these books. – And if his Majesty perused one through before breakfast – though it might spoil his appetite – yet the consciousness of having it in his power to facilitate the great work – would give an additional sweetness to his tea.'

Clothing also supplied Sancho with many sartorial turns of phrase. He complained to one correspondent that 'I could really write as long a letter on a taylor's measure, as your last hurry-begotten note.' He considered patience as basic a virtue as 'coat and lining'. Similarly, 'Humility should be the poor man's shirt – and thankfulness his girdle'.

These metaphors are especially poignant when one considers that all his life Sancho was forced by poverty to scrimp and save for such necessities as food and clothing. Many of Sancho's letters were written to thank the friends who had sent his family gifts of venison, pork chops, boxes of fruit, and even currant jelly. Like other servants in the Montagu household, most of Sancho's clothes were cast-offs. Only very occasionally did his master buy him new suits. During his dissolute period in the 1750s he is reputed to have gambled away his own clothes in a game of cribbage with a Jewish gentleman. In 1768 he was forced to beg John Meheux for cast-offs for his family who are 'very nearly in a state of nature in the article of covering... Mind, we ask no money – only rags – mere literal rags'.

Such passages embody the tension between art and commerce throughout Sancho's later years. He may have conversed with writers and painters, published musical compositions and dined with dramatists, but nothing would gloss over the fact that he was an impoverished and socially vulnerable negro living in a foreign land. It is interesting that one of Sancho's most emotional letters was his note of thanks to Meheux who, as requested, had sent his family various garments by return of post. Sancho trembled with happiness and gratitude. Claiming to be on the verge of tears, he quoted Othello, the fictional Moor whose life was wrecked by a planted handkerchief, and who, although 'unused to the melting mood', wept at the sight of Desdemona's corpse. It is the shared experience of being black, socially buffeted and on the verge of ruination because of (a lack of) cloth that connects these two characters across the centuries.

One of the most appealing aspects of Sancho's letters is his depiction of the comforts and tribulations of domestic life in the metropolis. We commonly read accounts of black people inhabiting the public sphere during the 18th century. On the one hand, they were used to adorn the arms and embody the wealth of aristocratic families. At another level, we regard the likes of Equiano and Naimbanna as very public performers. Their roles were political: they inveighed large audiences with accounts of the daily tortures wreaked on their black brethren toiling on the plantations. The tone of their books was often exhortatory, steeped in the codes of the public soapbox. Sancho himself, as we shall see later, was not afraid to make loud proclamations on social and political issues. Yet there is another equally important side to him. His letters often speak of his wife, his young children, leisurely family trips, a world beyond work and the selling of groceries and packets of tea.

Considering that women made up less than 20% of London's black population, Sancho's marriage to a West Indian, Anne Osborne, was most unusual. Even more uncommon was her literacy: we hear of her reading the newspaper or the letters that her husband was busy composing and which, on occasion, were signed on both their behalfs. Her brother, John, lived in Bond Street throughout the 1770s and the families clearly got on well with each other. In a bleak letter written after the death of his daughter, Kitty, Sancho told William Stevenson of how he hoped to come to terms with his grief: 'To-morrow night I shall have a few friends to meet brother Osborne, we intend to be merry'.

But such bleakness was the exception rather than the rule. Sancho's wife brought him great succour and joy. He refered to her jocularly as 'old Duchess', 'hen', and, together with their children, as 'My best half and Sanchonetta's'. Such affectionate pet names indicate a great sense of familial strength and unity. Life in London became unbearable without Anne. In a letter from Richmond, Sancho admitted to Meheux that 'I am heartily tired of the country; – the truth is – Mrs. Sancho and the girls are in town: – I am not ashamed to own that I love my wife – I hope to see you married, and as foolish.'

One might think such statements unworthy of comment. After all, they are the kind of amatory, affectionate phrases that are often found in love letters. Yet from Gronniosaw to Jean Rhys, Equiano to Hanif Kureishi, in two centuries of writing about London by African and South Asian writers, there are almost no other accounts of quiet, domestic contentment. This makes the Sanchos' married life in Westminster during the height of the Atlantic slave trade (a traffic which cleft African families so wickedly), and when slavery was still legal in England, all the more unusual. The fact that Ignatius led quite a public life – chatting with customers at his counter or the shop door, discoursing on cultural issues with contemporary artists, writing letters to newspapers – makes the unguarded, homely episodes in his letters all the more endearing.

There is a dazed intoxication in his letter of Friday 20 October 1775 to a Miss Leach for that very afternoon Anne had given birth: 'she has been very unwell for this month past – I feel myself a ton lighter: – In the morning I was crazy with apprehension – and now I talk nonsense tho' joy.' Avoiding pomposity, Sancho takes delight in the progress of this, his only son, William: 'he is the type of his father – fat – heavy – sleepy'. Later we learn of Billy's teething and his first few steps. But there is also a pensivity here. Sancho was in his late forties and appreciated how quickly he himself was declining in health. He seems to fear that he would not be around for much longer and this made him even more apprehensive than most parents are for their children: 'The girls are rampant well – and Bill gains something every day. – The rogue is to excess fond of me – for which I pity him – and myself more.' In the earlier letter recounting Billy's first steps, Sancho wondered if he should 'live to see him at man's estate' and prayed that 'God's grace should...ably support him through the quicksands, rocks, and shoals of life'.

According to Jekyll, Sancho's mother fell prey to a 'disease of the new climate' shortly after Ignatius had been baptised in Cartagena in Spanish America. Shortly afterwards his father committed suicide to avoid a life of servitude. Given the appalling circumstance of his parents' deaths, Sancho's assertions of domestic duty become all the more poignant: 'Say much for me to your good father and mother – in the article of respect thou canst not exaggerate – Excepting conjugal, there are no attentions so tenderly heart-soothing as the parental.'

Sancho certainly showered attention on his children. He took his daughters, Marianne and Betsy, to see John Henderson play Falstaff which they enjoyed greatly. On Marianne's sixteenth birthday her family feasted on goose and apple pie (the former donated by a friend). Ignatius both proudly and wistfully observed 'Her breast filled with delight unmixed with cares – her heart danced in her eyes – and she looked the happy mortal.' It is occasions such as these which justify Sancho's description of his home as a 'castle of peace and innocence'. The phrase suggests that 20 Charles Street was something of a retreat, a fortress to ward off the confusion and hardship outside.

It is gladdening to read of Sancho's efforts to ignore the threat of racial contumely and treat his children to the sights and smells of London. One evening 'three great girls – a boy – and a fat old fellow' eschewed travelling over Westminster Bridge in order to go, less prosaically, by boat to New Spring Gardens, near Lambeth Palace. Temporarily liberated from the anxieties of commerce, far away from the stench, ordure, fogs and clatter that filled the capital's busy streets, they luxuriated in this August idyll: '[they were] as happy and pleas'd as a fine evening – fine places – good songs – much company – and good music could make them. – Heaven and Earth! – how happy, how delighted were the girls!' It must have been rare for the family to enjoy such simple pleasures as these. No fee was charged for entering the Gardens, but Sancho lacked both the time and the money for transport that regular excursions such as this required. In any case, did his family always want to be objects of scrutiny for passers-by? The London mob often treated foreigners with contempt. On their way home from the Gardens, the Sanchos 'were gazed at – followed, &c. &c. – but not much abused.'

The note of incipient gloom that emerged when Sancho gazed affectionately at his children dangling at his knees and playing besides his puffed-up ankles was also never far away when he talked of 'Dame' Anne: 'If a sigh escapes me, it is answered by a tear in her eye. – I oft assume a gaiety to illume her dear sensibility with a smile – which twenty years ago almost bewitched me'. Their love never dwindled. It intensified in the face of Sancho's increasing enfeeblement. The last few letters he wrote are impossibly moving: 'I am now (bating the swelling of my legs and ancles) much mended – air and exercise is all I want – but the fogs and damps are woefully against me. – Mrs. Sancho ...reads, weeps, and wonders, as the various passions impel'. A week before his death we read, 'Mrs. Sancho, who speaks by her tears, says what I will not pretend to decypher'. It is an exhilarating moment in the history of black British literature: here is a rare assertion of passion, mutual dependancy, the hard-won intimacy between a formerly enslaved husband and his wife. It is also a chastening, grievous moment: Sancho is about to die; his children will lack a father and be further steeped in poverty. The domestic joy which these letters reveal was rare in 18th-century London. Nor did it abound during the next 200 years.

After Gronniosaw, Sancho was the second black cartographer of London, and stands at the head of a literary tradition that encompasses the likes of Equiano, Jean Rhys, V. S. Naipaul and Salman Rushdie. Many of his letters show his keenness for staying abreast of topical issues and contemporary metropolitan news. He wrote letters to the press; discoursed on painting and sculpture with artist friends; Gainsborough's friend, John Henderson, pressed Sancho to see him perform as Falstaff; Garrick dined with him; the composer and violinist, Felice Giardini, sent him tickets which Sancho passed onto a friend so that he might 'judge of fiddlers' taste and fiddlers' consequence in our grand metropolis'.

In December 1779 Sancho unsuccessfully applied to have his grocery serve as a post office: 'it would emancipate me from the fear of serving the parish offices – for which I am utterly unqualified through infirmities – as well as complexion'. It is those last four words which give this sentence such a sting in the tail. Sancho goes on to couch his proposal in a tone of comic amiability, and, in doing so, reveals a keen sense of how he might appear to his fellow Londoners. Yet there is no disguising the very real terror of having what little savings and social status he had accrued over the years suddenly snatched away from him by penury:

> Figure to yourself, my dear Sir, a man of a convexity of belly exceeding Falstaff – and a black face into the bargain – waddling in the van of poor thieves and pennyless prostitutes – with all the supercilious mock dignity of little office – what a banquet for wicked jest and wanton wit.

Some critics have cited such comments as proof that Sancho was embarrassed by his colour. On another occasion, Sancho bade a correspondent 'the prayers – not of a raving mad whig, nor fawning deceitful tory – but of a coal-black, jolly African'. In a fine letter condemning the mass dissipation and lawlessness of the 1780 Gordon Riots Sancho lambasted the 'worse than Negro barbarity of the populace' before concluding 'I am not sorry I was born in Afric'. But the point of all these examples is to show that they are attacks on failings in English social and political life. Sancho invoked his colour deliberately to satirise aspects of English society all the more devastatingly considering that it was him who was supposed to be a member of the immoral, savage and stupid negro race. The idea that Sancho sought to appease his correspondents is untenable. He exasperatedly lampooned common stereotypes about the black intellect: 'from Othello to Sancho the big – we are either foolish – or mulish – all – all without a single exception.' In a letter to Stevenson, he claimed that someone for whom he had performed many acts of charity may be wary of accepting such kindness 'from the hands of a poor negroe – (Pooh, I do not care for your prancings, I can see you at this distance)'. The parenthesis shows that Sancho had no time for any liberal reticence about admitting to and confronting the awkward exigencies of racial prejudice. The fact that he could call himself 'Sancho the big' or talk of the 'warm ebullitions of African sensibility' reveals again not only the playfulness that we saw earlier when exploring the literary texture of his writings but his relatively self-assured acceptance both of his colour and his anomalous position within English society.

During these latter years of economic insecurity, Sancho's mood was not helped by the fact that he felt himself to be surrounded by undeserved affluence and casual amorality. 'Trade is duller than ever I knew it – and money scarcer; – foppery runs higher – and vanity stronger; – extravagance is the adored idol of this sweet town.' He asked a friend in India to write to him of the 'customs – prejudices – fashions – and follies' of the people there – 'Alas! we have plenty of the two last here'. As we read through the *Letters*, there is a growing sense of the moral dissolution which was corroding the capital's soul. As a shopkeeper, Sancho had daily contact with many of the fops that he later criticised. He certainly felt that there had been a recent coarsening, a strident moral laxity amongst the people of London. In one of his bleakest and most vituperative letters, Sancho mourned that 'Trade is at so low an ebb...we are a ruined people'.

Sancho was an ardent royalist who lamented that 'it is too much the fashion to treat the Royal Family with disrespect.' He was further bruised by the economic and territorial wars that raged throughout the empire during the second half of the 1770s. At such times of flux Sancho often took refuge in his blackness; invoking his African birthright gave him a kind of spiritual and intellectual space in which to divorce himself from his awful surroundings:

> Ireland almost in as true a state of rebellion as America. – Admirals quarrelling in the West-Indies – and at home Admirals that do not choose to fight. – The British empire mouldering away in the West – annihilated in the North – Gibraltar going – and England fast asleep...For my part, it's nothing to me – as I am only a lodger – and hardly that.

Sancho may claim he is only a lodger but the mass of political details that he supplies in this last letter reveals someone who keeps scrupulously up-to-date with contemporary affairs. It is not the blasé or wilfully ignorant response of the genuinely detached lodger. After all, on another occasion 'Actuated by zeal to my prince, and love to my country' he wrote to *The General Advertiser* with a plan for reducing the national debt. Elsewhere, he referred to 'our righteous metropolis'. More likely, Sancho's exasperated outcry was borne of a desperation for quietude. Sancho's life had rarely been free from disruption and upheaval. Now, at the end of his days, all he wanted to do was to maintain his family and consolidate his grocery's finances. If he could also indulge in gossipation, or take some time to browse through the *Gazette* whilst reclining in his easy chair, occasionally gazing fondly at both his wife while she chopped sugar at a table and at his children playing near that fireplace over which stood a portrait of his friend, Mrs Cocksedge, then that would be as close to happiness in London as he could hope to achieve.

Sancho's reputation has flourished, dipped and risen again since the publication of the *Letters* in 1782. The first edition was a huge success: it attracted an almost

unprecedented 1,181 subscribers including the Prime
Minister, Lord North, and sold out within six months. The
press reaction was largely favourable. *The European
Magazine* claimed in 1782 that the book 'presents to us the
naked effusions of a negroe's heart, and shews it glowing
with the finest philanthropy, and the purest affections.
...They have more warmth than elegance of diction, and
more feeling than correctness'.

By the second half of the 1780s Sancho's *Letters* was
cited by the abolitionist movement as an outstanding
refutation of the idea that black people lacked souls,
intellects or rational faculties. Over the next couple of
decades Sancho was profiled and his correspondence
reprinted in various anthologies of negro biography and
literature compiled by English, French and American
abolitionists.

By the early 19th century Sancho had begun to seem a
rather mythical character, whose girth, learning and social
rank all exceeded the bounds of probability. The few
references to him usually speak of an 'extraordinary
literary character'. Slowly over the course of the next few
decades, Sancho became relegated to the status of a
fascinating footnote, an antiquarian's delight. In the course
of an 1888 article on antique tobacco labels, *Tobacco*
reproduced one of Sancho's trading cards. Reader response
must have been favourable for three months later the
magazine profiled Sancho as part of its 'Some Old
Tobacconists' series. Commending 'this very lovable man'
and 'the true nobility of his mind', the author of the article
compares Sancho to Johnson:

Physically, they were both corpulent and unwieldy in
their persons; intellectually, they were giants, their
minds ranging over a large area, and easily assimilating,
and quick to appreciate the characters and facts which
surround them. Socially, they were in their habits
domestic, and in their aspirations noble. Johnson,

however, had his biographer; it is regrettable that
Ignatius Sancho did not meet with his Boswell

('Gillespie', 1888b, p. 157).

This article raised the hackles of some readers. A certain
John Pickford wrote to *Notes and Queries* the following
year to complain that *Tobacco*'s reproduction of
Bartolozzi's engraving of Sancho 'represents a hideously
ugly black man...it certainly seems remarkable that an
eminent painter and engraver should have exercised their
talents upon him.'

Despite the occasional references to him in history
books and works of literary criticism in the first half of this
century, Sancho was largely forgotten until the end of the
1960s. Then, in the wake of decolonisation, there began to
emerge an increasing interest in the literary and cultural
achievements of African people throughout history. New
editions of Sancho's letters were published in London and
Ethiopia. However, as both English and African academics
carried out groundbreaking research into the black
presence in England before the 20th century, a rather
skewed picture of Sancho developed. Perhaps it was his
jowly face, perhaps the comedy that peppered his work,
but Sancho seemed too well-fed, too affluent and self-
assured to serve as an early dissident prophet. Equiano's
stridency was believed to be more likely to strike a chord
with black youths who, throughout the late 1970s and
early 1980s, felt especially embattled and buffeted by
unemployment, overzealous policing and a lack of social
services. To this day it is Equiano who is most likely to
appear in television series about black anti-imperialists, in
hip hop magazines, or on the cover of sociology journals
(although, as Reyahn King has shown, the portrait used on
these occasions is of somebody else altogether). It seems
that a subtle critical orthodoxy has developed about
Sancho. Unlike Equiano, he is not seen as an activist, a
militant, someone battling away on the frontline. Instead,

he is felt to be obsequious, assimilationist, an interesting historical character but hardly a black forefather that one can be proud of.

In the light of such a widespread but, as I hope to have demonstrated, fundamentally erroneous perception, it is especially pleasing to read the interesting interpretations of Sancho's life and work by contemporary British writers. The novelist, Caryl Phillips, for instance, has sought to locate Sancho, together with the likes of T. S. Eliot, Joseph Conrad and Doris Lessing, in a grand tradition of 'outsider' authors who have come to England over the centuries and who, exploiting the fresh perspectives that their cultural backgrounds permit them, have embarked on major experiments with literary form.

Phillips is not the only writer intrigued and beguiled by Sancho. In 'A City Visible But Unseen', a section of *The Satanic Verses* (1988), Salman Rushdie, who has always been fascinated in the subversive potential of storytelling, exhumes a number of narratives, historiographies and buried accounts about the black presence in London. Sancho's intelligence, his unexpected stature in the Georgian metropolis, his friendship with Sterne (one of Rushdie's favourite writers), his poisonous barbs against foppery and prejudice – make him an integral part of black London's long history. Together with dummies of the black Florence Nightingale, Mary Seacole, and Ukawsaw Gronniosaw, a wax model of Sancho seems to swerve and undulate amongst the sweaty, hyper, multiracial ravers giving it up at Club Hot Wax. Rushdie believes that Sancho and those other 'migrants of the past' are 'as much the living dancers' ancestors as their own flesh and blood'. In contrast, across the dance hall and 'bathed in evil green light, wax villains cower and grimace: Mosley, Powell, Edward Long'. Some critics may deem Sancho, like Saladin Chamcha, the horn-spouting protagonist of *The Satanic Verses*, a self-hating assimilationist, but, for Rushdie, he is as deserving and vital a forebear as today's urban youth could hope for.

Sancho's literary, as opposed to historical, significance is threefold. Firstly, unlike some black writers of the 18th century, Sancho did not require a helping hand to compose his work. The literary criticism and philosophical passages with which he striated his letters demonstrate that he was no slavish parroter of the English language. This fact, over and above the very existence of his book, forced proponents of negro inferiority such as Thomas Jefferson, who later became President of America, to reframe their arguments that blacks lacked the ability to intellectualise or write creatively.

Sancho was also the first black writer to appreciate how important form and structure are in contributing to the meaning of a literary work. Centuries before the likes of V. S. Naipaul and Wilson Harris, Sancho saw that the way an author organises his text – in his case, strewing the page with dashes and uneven punctuation – has certain social and philosophical implications. Sancho realised that it was not enough to hold radical views about the creative abilities of black people – one also had to express them in a novel and radical form. In doing so he emphasised the break he was making with conventional ways of seeing and thinking about the moral and intellectual status of the African.

Finally, it is the tone of Sancho's letters that makes them unique in the early history of black British literature. They are teasing, jokey, playful. They are often gentle and domestic. But they are also sententious, exclamatory and didactic. All in all, there is a richness of tone and register here which is far removed from the rather drier polemics of other slave writers. It is little wonder that one of Sancho's correspondents wrote to him to say how much warmer she felt after reading his letters to her. For all his tetchy conservatism, his textual antics, and his accounts of illness, domestic bereavements and penny-pinching poverty, people reading Sancho for the first time today will find his letters an equally gladdening and heart-swelling experience.

Bibliography

Braidwood, S. (1994), *Black Poor and White Philanthropists: London's Blacks and the Foundation of the Sierra Leone Settlement 1786–1791*, Liverpool Historical Studies, Liverpool: Liverpool University Press;

Brown, T. ([1700], 2nd edn., 1702): *Amusements Serious and Comical Calculated for the Meridian of London*, London;

Burr, S. and A. Potkay (eds) (1995), *Black Atlantic Writers of the Eighteenth Century: Living the New Exodus in England and the Americas*, Basingstoke: Macmillan;

Cash, A. (1975), *Laurence Sterne: The Early and Middle Years*, London: Methuen;

Cugoano, O. (1787), *Thoughts and Sentiments on the Evil and Wicked Traffic of the Slavery and Commerce of the Human Species*, London;

Curtis, L. P. (ed.) (1935), *Letters of Laurence Sterne*, Oxford: Clarendon Press;

Dickson, W. (1789), *Letters On Slavery*, London: J. Phillips;

Edwards, P. and J. Walvin (eds) (1983), *Black Personalities in the Era of the Slave Trade*, London: Macmillan;

Edwards, P. (1992), 'Unreconciled Strivings and Ironic Strategies: Three Afro-British Authors of the Georgian Era, Ignatius Sancho, Olaudah Equiano, Robert Wedderburn', *Occasional Papers* no. 34, Edinburgh: Centre of African Studies, Edinburgh University;

Edwards, P. and P. Rewt (eds) (1994), *The Letters of Ignatius Sancho*, Edinburgh: Edinburgh University Press;

Equiano, O. (1789), *The Interesting Narrative Of The Life Of Olaudah Equiano, Or Gustavus Vassa, The African. Written By Himself*, 2 vols, London;

The European Magazine, And London Review; Containing the Literature, History, Politics, Arts, Manners and Amusements of the Age. For September, 1782, London: J. Fielding, vol. 2, pp. 199–202;

Falk, B. (1958), *The Way of the Montagues: A Gallery of Family Portraits*, London: Hutchinson;

Fryer, P. (1984), *Staying Power. The History of Black People in Britain*, London: Pluto Press;

Gerzina, G. (1995), *Black England: Life Before Emancipation*, London: John Murray;

'Gillespie' (1888a), 'Some Old Tobacco Labels', in *Tobacco. A Monthly Trade Journal For The Importer, Exporter, Manufacturer, and Retailer of Tobacco*, [London], no. 86, 1 February 1888, pp. 36–8;

'Gillespie' (1888b), 'Some Old Tobacconists', in *Tobacco*, no. 90, 1 June 1888, pp. 156–8;

Grégoire, H. (1808), *De La Littérature Des Nègres, ou Recherches sur leurs facultés intellectuelles, leurs qualités morales et leur littérature; suivies de Notices sur la vie et les ouvrages des Nègres qui se sont distingués dans les Sciences, les Lettres et les Arts*, Paris;

Gronniosaw, U. (n.d. [1772]), *A Narrative of the Most Remarkable Particulars in the Life of James Albert Ukawsaw Gronniosaw, An African Prince, Written by Himself*, Bath: S. Hazard;

Hecht, J. J. (1956), *The Domestic Servant Class In Eighteenth-Century England*, London: Routledge and Kegan Paul;

Jefferson, T. ([1782] 1955), *Notes on the State of Virginia*, Institute of Early American History and Culture at Williamsburg, Virginia, Chapel Hill: University of North Carolina;

Long, E. (1774), *History of Jamaica. Or, General Survey Of the Ancient and Modern State Of That Island: With Reflections on its Situation, Settlements, Inhabitants, Climate, Products, Commerce, Laws and Government*, 3 vols, London: T. Lowndes;

[Macaulay, Z.] (n.d. [c.1797]), *The Black Prince, A True Story: Being An Account Of The life And Death of Naimbanna, An African King's Son, who arrived in England in the Year 1791, and set Sail on his Return in June*, 1793, London: J. Evans and Co.;

Mason, W. (1788), *An Occasional Discourse, Preached In The Cathedral of St. Peter In York, January 27, 1788. On The Subject of the African Slave Trade*, York: Printed by A. Ward for the Author;

Mott, A. (ed.) (1826), *Biographical Sketches And Interesting Anecdotes of Persons of Colour*, York: W. Alexander and Son;

Myers, N. (1996), *Reconstructing The Black Past. Blacks in Britain 1780–1830*, London: Frank Cass;

Notes and Queries (1858), [London], 2nd series, V, no. 123, 8 May 1858, p. 375;

Peckard, P. (1788), *Am I Not a Man? and a Brother? With All Humility Addressed To The British Legislature*, Cambridge: J. Archdeacon;

Phillips, C. (1995), 'Hard times of the "outside" writers', *The Daily Telegraph*, 11 November 1995, p. A3;

Pickford, J. (1889), letter to *Notes and Queries*, 7th series, VIII, 13 July 1889, p. 33;

Rushdie, S. (1988), *The Satanic Verses*, London: Viking;

Sandiford, K. A. (1988), *Measuring the Moment: Strategies of Protest in Eighteenth-Century Afro-English Writing*, Selinsgrove: Susquehanna University Press;

Shepherd, T. B. (1940), *Methodism and the Literature of The Eighteenth Century*, London: The Epworth Press;

Sterne, L. ([1759–1767] 1983), *The Life and Opinions of Tristram Shandy, Gentleman*, Oxford: Clarendon Press;

Sterne, L. ([1760] 1927), *Philanthropy Recommended, reprinted in The Sermons of Mr Yorick*, vol. 1, Oxford: Basil Blackwell for The Shakespeare Head Press of Stratford-Upon-Avon;

Sypher, W. (1942), *Guinea's Captive Kings: British Anti-Slavery Literature of the XVIIIth Century*, Chapel Hill: The University of North Carolina Press;

Voltaire, F. de ([1728] 1807), *The Henriade*, London: William Sancho;

Wordsworth, W. ([1850] 1985), *The Fourteen-Book Prelude*, The Cornell Wordsworth Series, Ithaca: Cornell University Press.

PLATES

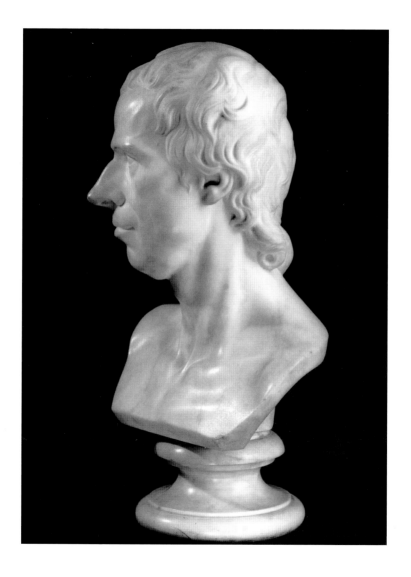

Figure 2
Francis Williams, *c.* 1700– *c.* 1770
By an unknown artist, *c.* 1740
Oil on canvas, 66 x 50.2 cm
© The Board of Trustees, Victoria and Albert Museum

TASTE IN HIGH LIFE.

Figure 3
Taste in High Life
After William Hogarth, 1746
Engraving, 29.2 x 21.6 cm
© The British Museum

Figure 4
Lady Mary Churchill, Duchess of Montagu (1689–1751), with Charles, her page
Attributed to Enoch Seeman, 1720s
Oil on canvas, 141.5 x 114.3 cm
© Boughton House

Figure 5
Louise de Kéroualle, Duchess of Portsmouth, 1649–1734
By Pierre Mignard, 1682
Oil on canvas, 120.7 x 95.3 cm
© National Portrait Gallery (497)

Figure 6
A Black Servant Carrying a Tray
By Hendrick Pothoven
Black and white chalk, 33 x 21.6 cm
© Agnew's

A MUNGO MACARONI.

Figure 9
Dido Elizabeth Belle, later Davinier and Lady Elizabeth Murray, later Finch Hatton
Attributed to Johann Zoffany, *c*. 1780
Oil on canvas, 119.4 x 139.7 cm
© Courtesy of the Earl of Mansfield

Figure 10
Study of a Black Man
By Sir Joshua Reynolds, *c.* 1770
Oil on canvas, 78.7 x 65 cm
© The Menil Collection, Houston

Figure 11
Portrait of a Black Man (Olaudah
Equiano, *c.* 1745–1797)
English School, 18th century
Oil on canvas, 61.8 x 51.5 cm
© Royal Albert Memorial
Museum, Exeter

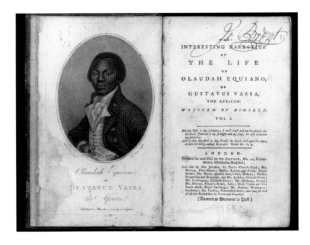

Figure 12
Frontispiece from *The Interesting Narrative of
the Life of Olaudah Equiano or Gustavus Vassa, the African*
By Olaudah Equiano (*c.* 1745–1797), first edition, 1789
Engraved by D. Orme after W. Denton
© Private Collection

Figure 13
George Augustus Polgreen
Bridgetower, 1778–1860
By Henry Edridge, 1837, inscribed
by previous owner, G. Fossey
Pencil and watercolour,
18.4 x 21.3 cm (oval)
© The British Museum

Figure 14
A Musical Club (including what is thought to be the figure of Joseph Antonia Emidy)
By an unknown artist, inscribed and dated 'Two, 8 November 1808'
Watercolour, 26 x 18.7 cm
Reproduced with the permission of the Royal Institution of Cornwall

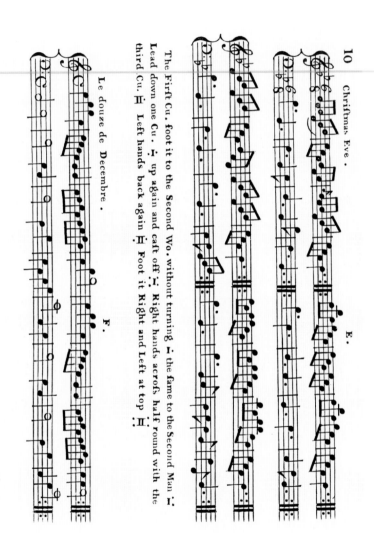

Figure 15
'Christmas Eve' and 'Le douze Decembre' from: *Minuets, Cotillons and Country Dances for the Violin, Mandolin, German-Flute, & Harpsichord (with obligato French horn parts)*
By Ignatius Sancho, *c.* 1767
Printed engraved plate, oblong quarto size
© The British Library

Figure 16
'The Sweetest Bard' from: *A Collection of New Songs*
By Ignatius Sancho, *c.* 1769
Broadsheet, 32.5 x 21.5 cm
© The British Library

Mr Garrick reciting the Ode, in honor of Shakespeare, at the Jubilee at Stratford; with the Musical Performers &c.

Figure 17
Mr Garrick reciting the Ode in honor of Shakespeare
at the Jubilee at Stratford, with the Musical Performers
Coloured engraving, 12.7 x 18.9 cm
© National Portrait Gallery (Archive)

Chapter 3

Ignatius Sancho: The Man and His Times

James Walvin

Ignatius Sancho was born a slave in 1729, to a slave mother (who died shortly afterwards) on board an Atlantic slave ship heading for the Americas. At the time of Sancho's birth, the British had become the most successful and most prosperous of European slave-traders. Though that maritime trade in Africans was initiated by the Spaniards and Portuguese, and developed by the Dutch, it was perfected by the British. The British shipped more people than any other nation, transforming the enslavement of Africans, and their sale in the Americas, into a major commercial operation. On the backs of imported slaves – and of their locally-born descendants – the British waxed prosperous. Trade and profit flowed from the Caribbean sugar islands and from the tobacco colonies of the Chesapeake. Sugar transformed the nation's tastes, sweetening the newly acquired passion for tea, coffee and chocolate, while tobacco provided those familiar rituals of manly sociability in the tavern and coffee house. From elaborate tea-drinking rituals in fashionable homes, to the sharing of cheap, re-used tea leaves among the labouring poor, British social life was reshaped by products of distant empires. When we look at the flow of material benefits and profits from the enslaved Americas it is hard to imagine British life without slavery. Its social and economic benefits had seeped into most corners of the nation. But the human cost of these profits and pleasures was a catastrophe visited upon large regions of Africa, and upon those Africans violently scattered around the edges of the British Atlantic slave system. There were millions, like Sancho's mother, who were plucked from African homelands to toil in the Americas.

It is tempting to think that the slaves' efforts – on the far side of the Atlantic – were out of sight and therefore out of mind. Yet Sancho's life is a reminder that the slave experience was often more obvious and direct than we might sometimes imagine. For a start Sancho, like many other slaves and black domestics, made his home in Britain. In the course of the 18th century a noticeable black community developed, especially in London, a reminder of Atlantic slavery itself and of the more sizeable black communities in the Americas. All was made possible by British maritime trade and commerce. During the course of the 18th century, some 11,000 ships left Britain (one half of them from Liverpool, the rest mainly from Bristol, London and Glasgow), for the 'triangular trade' to Africa and thence to the Americas. The slave trade was thought to be so lucrative that even the smallest and remotest of ports dispatched ships to trade in African humanity; from Poole and Lyme Regis, from Lancaster and Whitehaven. The ports thrived, and so too did their immediate economic hinterlands, as produce and manufactured goods from inland regions and towns filled the departing slave ships. Metalwares from Birmingham and the West Country, textiles from Yorkshire and Lancashire, foodstuffs from Scotland and Ireland, commodities crafted by workmen from the length and breadth of Britain, all found their way to the African coast and to the slave plantations of the Americas. It was a massive, expansive (though generally risky) trade, whose profits silenced any isolated voice of moral objection.

Like millions of others, Ignatius Sancho inherited his mother's slave status – to be bought, sold, bartered and bequeathed – and all in order to tap the wealth of the Americas for European gain. Something in the region of eleven million Africans were landed in this way, the very great bulk of them destined for the sugar colonies. Many others simply did not survive, either on the trade routes within Africa or on the horrific sea crossing. Given the vast numbers involved, it was inevitable that some, like Sancho, would find their way to Britain.

Sancho was brought to Britain as a small child, where he worked for three sisters in Greenwich. This was the period when fashion decreed the use of black domestics, both enslaved and free. In the homes of wealthy Londoners, fashionable spas and stately homes, black pages or servants were commonplace, a fact amply confirmed in any number of 18th-century portraits. Black servants were trained in the domestic skills and social graces expected by their owners and were often dressed in elaborate (sometimes bizarre) attire, both to catch the eye and to impress visitors and friends. Sancho was one such. Like other blacks, he also took the opportunity to improve himself, with the help of friends and the support of those who had noticed his abilities and industry. The Duke of Montagu, who spotted early on his potential, gave him books and Sancho quickly took to studying. But, to the horrified disapproval of his female owners, he also loved female company. At the age of twenty Sancho ran away from the sisters, seeking refuge in the Montagu household. There, working as a butler, he flourished, reading voraciously, writing prose, poetry and music. He became an avid theatre-goer and a fan of Garrick and became a figure in fashionable London society – friendly with actors, painters and, most interestingly, with Laurence Sterne.

By the late 1760s Sancho had made the progression from being a decorative black domestic to a man of refinement and accomplishment, penning letters to friends and sympathisers around the country. In 1773 he quit the life of a domestic servant and set up as a shopkeeper in Westminster, thanks to a small allowance bequeathed by the Duke of Montagu. With this modest backing, Sancho moved into a shop in Charles Street, Westminster, with his black wife Anne and their expanding family, eventually of six children whom he affectionately called his 'Sanchonettas'.

Such shops were relatively simple and cheap affairs. An investment of a mere £10 could yield an annual income of £50, and though London – especially Oxford Street – quickly established a reputation for its dazzling array of extravagant shops, much more typical was the humble local store, often little more than a counter in a front room, such as Sancho acquired. By the end of the 18th century, there were more than 20,000 shops like these in London. The basic trade was in sugar, tea and tobacco – all intimately linked to slavery of course.

As Sancho tended to his counter and customers – taking tea with favoured or famous clients – his wife Anne worked in the background, breaking down the sugar loaves into the smaller parcels and packets required for everyday use. Slave-grown sugar, repackaged and sold by black residents of London, themselves descendants of slaves – here was a scene rich in the realities and the symbolism of Britain's slave-based empire. Among the prominent visitors to Sancho's shop was Charles James Fox, leader of contemporary parliamentary radicals. We know that Sancho voted for Fox at the 1780 election, having acquired the right to vote by his property rights as a shopkeeper in Westminster. From what we know of Sancho's views, it is not surprising that he voted for Fox, but it is surely remarkable that at the high watermark of British slavery a black should cast a vote in a British election.

In the increasingly competitive world most 18th-century shopkeepers promoted their wares in various ways: through advertisements in their windows, above their doors and in local handbills and newspapers. Sancho was no exception. He also used a trade card, depicting his most important commercial item – tobacco. His card provides a telling picture, portraying all those elements of tobacco production which proved it so exploitative for so many people. It contains images of an American Indian, and of black slaves gathering the tobacco. On closer inspection, however, the image of slave work looks much more like slaves gathering sugar than tobacco. Yet the precision of the image is not the key point. What matters is the message. Here was a product – tobacco – which was brought forth by slaves for the pleasure and profit of Europeans, and was sold by an ex-slave shopkeeper in London. Sancho's trade card is another reminder, if we need one, of the centrality of slavery to 18th-century British trade commerce and prosperity.

The ironic images of slavery were there for all to see, and could be caught in other scenes of British domesticity. Black servants carried the tea services, including the sugar bowls, and fetched their masters' pipes, just as their contemporaries toiled in the fields in distant colonies to bring forth those same natural products. It was also customary for slave ships to carry pipes and tobacco to distribute to, and to pacify, African slaves as they crossed the Atlantic. Tobacco was also used to fumigate the holds of the slave ships. Yet who produced the tobacco in the first place?

Ignatius Sancho is better known as a correspondent than as a shopkeeper. He made himself known to men and women of sensibility throughout the country. He contacted Laurence Sterne, for example, to praise his work, and to bring to Sterne's attention the plight of enslaved Africans. In fact, Sterne had already taken up the issue. Moreover, the problems of slavery had already surfaced in a series of celebrated slave cases in English courts and newspapers. In the year Sancho was born, 1729, an important legal ruling had issued from the Attorney and Soliciter Generals following a petition from West India interests, concerned about their rights over slaves imported into England. The law officers decreed that: 'a slave, by coming from the West Indies, either with or without his master, to Great Britain or Ireland, doth not become free…We are also of opinion, that the master may legally compel him to return to the plantations.'

For some years past, English law had wrestled with the legal and social problems created by the movements of slaves from the Americas to Britain. Were slaves freed when they landed in a free land; were they free when baptised? Or did their enslaved status – confirmed by a host of parliamentary acts governing the colonies and the slave trade – remain applicable to Britain?

Twenty years later, in 1749, the Lord Chancellor, Lord Hardwicke, reaffirmed the earlier York/Talbot judgement; ruling that slavery *was* legally sanctioned in England. He ruled that the common belief that, 'the moment a slave sets foot in *England* he becomes free, has no weight with it, nor can any reason be found, why they should not be equally so when they set foot in *Jamaica*, or any other *English* plantation'. Yet judgement continued to be confused, and other judges made contrary rulings. Of course the legal fraternity was aware that any definitive freeing of slaves in Britain would form a breach in the previously secure British slave system. If slaves were to be freed in Britain, why not in the colonies? But those slave colonies continued to be the hub of unquestioned British material well-being; remove slavery which underpinned those colonies, and British economic interests would be damaged.

In practice slavery *did* exist in Britain and could be seen in the number of slave sales and slave runaways announced in 18th-century newspapers. How could it be otherwise, with such large-scale movements of people and ships between the African slave coast, the slave colonies of the Americas, and Britain? Not surprisingly, then, Africans and American-born blacks began to appear throughout Britain. Most, however, found themselves in London; the heart of Britain's maritime empire and the centre of the political and social culture which sustained Atlantic slavery and all that flowed from it.

Sancho was, then, one of many blacks in 18th-century Britain, though precisely how many remains uncertain. Yet it is clear enough that these reluctant black settlers in London developed into a genuine community. Black servants and slaves gravitated towards each others' company, meeting in the homes of their masters, in their favourite local tavern, celebrating together and, most crucially, passing on news and information which reached them from the dockside and from the slave colonies of the Americas. It was here, in the black community, that voices were raised against slavery.

Though criticisms of slavery were few in the early 18th century, by the 1760s a small band of critics in London – men of sensibility horrified by what they learnt of slavery – began to raise their doubts. Some of what they learnt about slavery was often gleaned from blacks living in London. Granville Sharp, a government clerk, began to agitate and write against slavery after 1765, following a chance discovery of cruelties inflicted on slave servants in London. Sharp researched into their legal status and, anxious to defend them, realised that the best way to ensure their freedom in England, to prevent their enforced return to the colonies, was to secure writs of habeas corpus on their behalf. This formed the genesis of the broader (and better known) British campaign against slavery. And in all this, the experiences and information of local, British-based blacks proved crucial.

Ignatius Sancho had already added his voice to the campaign against slavery. And the voice of an ex-slave had a resonance all its own. His most effective role was that of quiet agitator, raising the issue of slavery – the sufferings of what he called the 'thousands of my brother Moors' – with his various correspondents. More eye-catching, in the short term however, was the agitation of Granville Sharp, which culminated (but did not end) in the well-known – though often misunderstood – Somerset case of 1772. Sharp sought to prevent a slave's enforced removal back to the Caribbean by securing a writ of habeas corpus (i.e. forcing the slave owner to justify before a court the detention of the slave). Mansfield, the Lord Chief Justice, aware that his decision had major implications for the slave lobby, was hesitant and slow to decide. But his judgement, delivered on 22 June 1772, was a turning point. Mansfield ruled that no-one had the authority to remove a slave from England against his/her wishes: 'No master ever was allowed here to take a slave by force to be sold abroad because he deserted from his service, or for any other reason whatsoever'.

He did *not* decide, however, that slavery was illegal in England, though many continued to believe it was. As if to confirm the point, advertisements for slaves continued to appear in English newspapers, as did infamous cases of pursuit and capture of runaway slaves. Whatever the limitations of the 1772 Mansfield verdict, London's blacks – a group of whom were present throughout the Somerset hearings – celebrated in some style. It was a limited, partial victory, secured by a unique political/legal alliance of black and white. Yet it left much to be done. What dawned on that small band of white anti-slavery supporters (which found a focus in the remarkable, influential Quaker community) was that nothing less than black freedom *tout court* (i.e. an end to the British slave empire itself) could resolve the matter.

In the decade before his death in late 1780, Sancho, now in his forties, became an inveterate letter-writer. He had made earlier attempts at writing but his subsequent reputation was founded in the letters he penned in the 1770s. Was it mere accident that the very great majority of his letters were drafted when he had quit domestic service and had become a shopkeeper? Or perhaps the life of a simple grocer allowed Sancho the time and circumstances to dispatch letters to all and sundry, prompted no doubt by that world of political and polite gossip which passed through his shop. He was now party to a social world previously denied him as a domestic. The status of servitude had been left behind and Sancho was free to communicate directly with customers, and in his spare moments by letter with distant correspondents. The nature and style of his letters suggest that Sancho had disciplined himself in a style he thought appropriate for the intended correspondents, and there seems little doubt that his basic literary style was greatly influenced by Laurence Sterne.

Sancho's reputation as a letter-writer had first been established by the publication of Sterne's own letters in 1775. Sancho's initial contact with Sterne (in 1766) had been to praise *Tristram Shandy* in a letter which mixed praise with excessive sentimentality. From the first, Sancho described himself as 'one of those people whom the vulgar and illiberal call '*Negurs*.'; a man whose feelings were aroused by Sterne's own barbs against slavery: 'Of all my favourite authors, not one has drawn a tear in favour of my miserable black brethren – excepting yourself and the humane author of Sir George Ellison.' Sancho urged Sterne to speak out on behalf of 'the uplifted hands of thousands of my brother Moors'. Sterne's response to Sancho's elaborate approaches seems to have encouraged the subsequent wave of letters which Sancho dispatched right and left, once he had more time on his hands as a shopkeeper. These letters form a rare insight into the life and times of an ex-slave living in 18th-century England.

Sancho's writings provide much more than a glimpse of an interesting, if distinctive, late 18th-century figure. They take us to the very heart of the black experience at the height of the enslaved African diaspora. Time and again, Sancho speaks about – speaks for – his fellow Africans, and about slavery 'as it is at this time practiced in our West Indies'. But Sancho also spoke about the fate of the British black community, a community which was itself forged by slavery. The sole reason for the black presence in Britain was the Atlantic slave system. Blacks arrived in Britain as a consequence of the movement of Africans into the Americas. People returning from the slave colonies – planters, officials, soldiers, as well as the sailors on the slave ships – often returned home with personal slaves. But as the 18th century advanced, it proved more difficult to maintain control over slaves in England, especially in London. Sancho himself was a case in point. With the passage of time many were lured away by local free blacks, or were freed by their owners. We do not know how many, or what proportion, of the British black population were slaves and how many were free. Yet slave owners regularly tried to take black domestics back to the slave colonies against their will. Indeed it was such incidents which provided the early abolitionists led by Granville Sharp with their first breakthrough in the campaign against slavery. Slavery in England itself continued, however, sustained, as before, by the movement of peoples back and forth across the Atlantic and by the continuing use of slavery in British colonies.

For much of the 18th century, as the material bounty yielded by slavery increased and diversified, any initial worries about the ethics of slavery were simply swamped.

What would Glasgow have been without tobacco; how would Liverpool have fared without the slave trade? Economic self-interest simply overwhelmed whatever moral scruples contemporaries might have had about the enslavement of legions of Africans and about their immiseration on the far side of the Atlantic. It was a process which distance rendered more comfortable for the British. But the evolution of a black community in London, and the legal difficulties periodically thrown up by slave cases in English (and Scottish) courts, ensured that the broader problem of slavery became progressively more troublesome. Blacks in Britain, the slave cases in courts, the occasional black voice raised in anger – all this and more determined that the problem of slavery would not go away. It was this domestic British debate about slavery which formed the genesis of the early campaign against slavery. Although the Quakers had been opposed to slavery since the late 17th century, they remained, despite their growing commercial power, a marginalised sect with little overt political influence. The first people in Britain to ponder and agitate effectively how best to undermine the Atlantic slave system became aware of the problem by events and individuals in Britain itself. It was the black British slave, the black British voice – the lot and the fate of blacks living in Britain – which made the first important dint in the previously untroubled defences of the West Indian slave system.

In this, Ignatius Sancho played an important role. Always willing to raise the question of slavery with his friends and acquaintances, his letters touched on the plight of Africans everywhere and of the problems facing blacks in Britain. At times Sancho was open – even extravagant – in promoting the black cause. His letters to Sterne were perhaps the most blatant example of this mode of address, though he may have adopted Sterne's exaggerated mode of expression to make a point – 'Consider slavery – what it is – how bitter a draught – and how many have been made to drink of it!' More usual, however, was Sancho's passing references to the black experience; throwaway remarks about the occasional racial slur, the public insult and contemporary racist culture. Describing a family night out in London, he wrote: 'we went by water – had a coach home – were gazed at – followed, &c. &c. – *but not much abused*.' [my emphasis]

Why should Sancho make such a point? Why describe something which had *not* happened – except to show that the opposite was much more common? Sancho regularly reminded his correspondents about the abuse blacks were likely to receive in public. He reminded Soubise, another African servant (to the Duchess of Queensberry), of the 'ill-bred and heart-racking abuse of the foolish vulgar'. At one point, despite a lifetime in England, Sancho described himself as: 'a lodger – and hardly that.' At times he clearly despaired: 'to the English, from Othello to Sancho the big – we are either foolish – or mulish – all – all without a single exception.'

Like his fellow blacks, Sancho could not avoid the periodic barbs of hostile, vulgar abuse, much of it directed at his colour. In private letters, however, he sometimes turned this on its head, revelling in his racial difference and taking as a badge of pride what others used as an insult. In his late years, as he grew fatter, he described himself as 'a man of a convexity of belly exceeding Falstaff' but adding, 'and a black face into the bargain'. In another letter he spoke of being 'a coal-black, jolly African'. At other times he described himself as 'a poor Blacky grocer' and 'only a poor thick-lipped son of Afric'. This jocularity in letters to his friends (to whom he sent 'Blackamoor greetings') never dimmed his sense of the wrongs done to unknown armies of his fellow Africans; 'my brother Negroes'. Nor did Sancho lose his sense of indignation of what Britain had done – and continued to do – to native peoples in Africa and other parts of the globe. And all for the pursuit of money: 'The grand object of English navigators – indeed of all Christian navigators – is money – money – money'. In pursuing this global commercial greed, the British had been 'uniformly wicked in the East – the West Indies – and even on the coast of Guinea'.

Understandably, Sancho was especially grieved about the fate of Africa and its slaves ('a subject that sours my blood') but he also blamed African rulers as well as European traders for the evils visited upon the continent: 'the Christians' abominable Traffic for slave – and the horrid cruelty and treachery of the petty Kings'.

From his first letter to Sterne in 1766 until his death fourteen years later, slavery hovered over Sancho's correspondence. And it was precisely in these same years that the question of slavery began that long complex process of gestation as a political and ethical issue in Britain, driven forward by a small band of indefatigable abolitionists and aided by the experiences of London's black community.

After years of apparent indifference, anti-slavery was launched by the slave cases in English courts and by the attendant publicity and controversy. The campaign to secure black freedom in Britain, though fought initially on a narrowly defined front, had major implications for the slave empires. The West India lobby, long prominent in London as political and economic spokesmen and lobbyists for slave-traders and planters, indeed for all involved in Atlantic slave trading, began to appreciate that their position was under threat. There thus began that political and publishing skirmishing – pitching friends of black freedom against supporters of the slave-trading lobby – which was to continue, with varying degrees of intensity, for the next fifty years.

The cause of black freedom needed the periodic injection of publicity. Events conspired to bring home to the British public the scale and the horror of life – and death – on the slave ships and in the slave colonies. Outrages against slaves were skilfully manipulated by emergent abolitionist groups, but nothing could exaggerate the murderous details of slavery itself. A year after Sancho's death, events on board a Liverpool ship, the *Zong*, surpassed even the worst stories purveyed by the abolitionists. In September 1781, the *Zong* left Africa bound for Jamaica with a large cargo of African slaves. By the end of November more than sixty slaves and seven of the crew had died. Many other slaves were sick and seemed doomed. The master, Luke Collingwood, decided to throw overboard those slaves who were likely to die, and to claim them as an insurance loss; slaves who died 'naturally' formed a simple commercial loss for the ship's backers. Collingwood selected 133 sick Africans, and the crew threw them overboard in batches. Despite some resistance (one slave managed to clamber back on board, another ten threw *themselves* overboard), over three days they were all killed. To compound this outrage, the ship's owners subsequently claimed for the deaths on their insurance, alleging that only by jettisoning the sick was it possible to maintain enough water to save the healthy, and the crew. In fact the ship arrived in Jamaica with more than 400 spare gallons of water. The insurance underwriters refused to pay – and thus the case surfaced as another legal dispute which hinged on the question of slavery.

Even by the standards of a society apparently immune to the horrors of slavery, the *Zong* caused an outcry. Granville Sharp – primed for any further slave cases which might advance his earlier argument against slavery in England – was alerted to the case by Olaudah Equiano, the African later to establish himself as the most prominent black spokesman in Britain. Here was proof of the link between black and white which was to become increasingly important as the campaign for black freedom developed on both sides of the Atlantic. When the *Zong* case came to court, the case was simply stated by the Soliciter-General:

> This is a case of chattels or goods. It is really so; it is the case of throwing over goods; for to this purpose, and the purpose of the insurance, they are goods and property: whether right or wrong, we have nothing to do with it.

Granville Sharp had other ideas, attending the hearing and determined to publicise both the murderous event and to expose the sanitised posturings of those English legal officials who claimed, throughout, that the incident was not a question of mass murder.

Despite persistent pressure and lobbying at the highest level, no action was taken against the men who perpetrated this crime. To raise the *principle* of African deaths and sufferings in an English court, was to expose the very heart of slavery itself. If every death, torture, brutality or outrage against Africans on board a British vessel, or on a plantation, were to find its way to court, the legal system would rapidly grind to a halt. And so too would the lucrative slave system itself. It was, after all, an economic system which needed Africans to be uprooted from their homelands and cultures, reduced, for the sake of British utility, to the level of chattel, and stripped – in law if not in social reality – of their humanity. The threats by Granville Sharp and his growing band of friends to use the law to secure the rights of blacks living in England, though narrowly focused was, potentially, corrosive of the whole Atlantic system.

The *Zong* case seems simply to have faded from English courts. But the details made a lasting impression and it heralded the awakening of political opinion to the wider problems of the British slave trade. What brought the issue into focus was the aftermath of the American War of Independence (1776–1783). As that war lapped through the North American slave colonies, the loyalty of local slaves was crucial to both sides in the conflict. The British had periodically used slaves in the fighting and as support labourers (often linked to the promise of freedom). When the defeated British finally quit, they escaped north to Canada or back to Britain with those former slaves who had sided with them in the war. These 'black loyalists' formed the origins of new black communities in Canada; those sailing to Britain swelled the ranks of London's 'black poor'. The commissioners dealing with claims for compensation for losses in that fighting looked much less favourably on black claims. The investigating commissioners felt that it was sufficient that the supplicant blacks had secured their freedom. But most of them slid quickly into abject poverty, their numbers sufficient to prompt a debate in 1785 in the English press about their condition.

In 1786 a committee was formed to provide relief for London's black poor and within months more than 400 had been provided with food, clothing or lodging. Bit by bit, the government was drawn in to solve the 'problem' of the black poor. There evolved a bungled and disastrous scheme to encourage London's blacks to return 'home' to Sierra Leone. Not surprisingly, only a relatively small number took up the offer of repatriation, not least because Sierra Leone was not in any sense 'home' to London's black population. The greatest fear was that resettlement was in the heart of the slave-trading region. In the words of an African resident in London, 'can it be readily conceived that government would establish a free colony for them nearly on the spot, while it supports its forts and garrisons, to ensnare, merchandize, and to carry others into captivity and slavery.' Groups of blacks organised and protested and Olaudah Equiano – the most prominent African used by the government to liaise with the black community – struggled to make black anxieties known to the organisers.

When the convoy sailed in April 1787 it carried only 350 blacks. Some 300 landed in Sierra Leone, to face a litany of disasters which were no less awful for having been predicted. Four years later, a mere sixty survived. Later, under a new scheme, more than 1,100 black loyalists quit their temporary refuge in Nova Scotia for Sierra Leone; this settlement thrived and formed the basis for the modern state of Sierra Leone. But the problems of London's black community could not be solved by the efforts to 'repatriate' them. Knots of poor blacks were to characterise the expanding city of London throughout the late 18th century. Periodically their plight surfaced, usually when yet another slave case broke surface in an English court and in the press. But by then the political climate had begun to change.

Late 18th-century Britain remained wedded to a slave-owning culture. But that culture found itself progressively attacked and undermined by evermore powerful forces. The legal and published debate initiated by Granville Sharp had taken off in the 1770s and 1780s, periodically stimulated by news of fresh outrages, or by the most recent legal dispute about slavery. The Abolition Society, launched in 1787, in the immediate wake of the *Zong* case and the Sierra Leone scheme, was dominated initially by Quakers, with their own nationwide network of contacts which formed the framework for the rapid growth of abolition throughout the country. Abolitionist petitions flooded Parliament in the 1780s and 1790s. One petition from the emergent textile town of Manchester contained more than 10,000 names. By the mid-1790s more than 500 petitions from across the country demanded an end to the slave trade. The intellectual roots of anti-slavery reached back to the writings of the French Enlightenment. But after 1789 the movement was galvanised by the ideas of the French Revolution. The concept of the 'Rights of Man' transformed the wider debate about human and political rights – for black and white, for men and women, and was promoted by a vast flow of cheap publications – among them writings by black authors. Abolitionists pressed home the attack, arguing in Parliament that abolishing the Atlantic slave trade would bring the end of slavery in the Americas a little closer. Progress was hindered by the excesses of the French Revolution. But abolition was driven forward by massive public agitation, in print, in crowded local meetings and through a visual and material culture of anti-slavery; in pictures, prints, plaques, medallions and pottery. Some of that material left a permanent mark on the collective British memory, notably the plan of the Liverpool slave ship, the *Brookes*, and Wedgwood's medallion of the kneeling slave – 'Am I not a Man and a Brother?'

Throughout this campaign the slaves played a key part.

Their collective voice was heard – and heeded – as never before. Black writers found their work adding to the groundswell of abolitionist sentiment. It was at this point that Ignatius Sancho found a posthumous fame and influence. His letters had been collected and published two years after his death, in 1782. Over the next twenty years they were reprinted five times (ensuring handsome royalties to his widow, who continued to run his Westminster shop). It was a book which brought a tone of educated civility to the abolition debates. Here was an African – an ex-slave – confronting contemporaries on terms they recognised and admired. Literate, sophisticated (however stylised), Sancho provided evidence of black attainment and potential. In a world grown accustomed to thinking of the African as a beast of burden, suited only to the physical demands of colonial labour, Sancho's cultural and literary style caught the eye. Nor was he alone.

The abolition activists clearly appreciated the importance of employing black activists and writers in their campaign. One was Ottobah Cugoano, another London-based African, who added his personal experience to the abolition cause in a book first published in 1787. Cugoano pushed the abolitionist case further than anyone else to date. He demanded total black freedom – not just an end to the slave trade – and the employment of the Royal Navy to prevent further slave trading. The most prominent and best remembered African abolitionist of these years was, however, Olaudah Equiano, whose memoirs of 1789 quickly became *the* African text in English in these years. His *Interesting Narrative* rapidly became a best-seller, its author soon established as the best known African in Britain, campaigning with radical friends in London and with abolitionist colleagues throughout Britain, to add the voice of personal experience to the broader abolitionist agitation. It is fitting that his book sells better today than ever before.

Equiano and Cugoano were friends and clearly worked together on their writing. Along with Sancho they formed a triumvirate of African writers whose personal experience of slavery infused abolition with an incalculable force. Their publications were utterly different. Sancho was the most polished – posed even; Cugoano a simpler, rougher voice; Equiano the more politically alert and specific. Yet Sancho's remained the most curious volume, not least because it was posthumous. But Sancho's letters were important in being able to appeal precisely to the people abolition needed to woo: the educated, the propertied and the influential.

The swelling tide against slavery was inspired of course by a host of factors. Slaves in the West Indies played a key role in loosening their own chains, most spectacularly in a series of slave revolts, led by the successful slave revolution in Haiti (St. Domingue). At the same time more and more people began to doubt the previously unquestioned economic benefits of slavery. New economic orthodoxies, notably a debate about free trade (prompted primarily by Adam Smith's *Wealth of Nations* in 1776), disputed the protected economic system which buttressed slavery. Moreover, as the British economy changed and moved into the early phases of industrialisation, there were many other opportunities beckoning investors; opportunities which lacked the dangers (and the moral problems) of the slave system. Thus it was, by the early 19th century, that morality and economic utility began to unite in an increasingly strident campaign against slavery itself.

The slave trade was ended in 1807. Though slavery survived in the British West Indies for another thirty years, to more and more people it seemed a throw-back to a bygone world; a grotesque contrast to contemporary British economic and social values and a stain on the British character. When the British finally ended colonial slavery, between 1834 and 1838, they changed tack dramatically, henceforth boasting about their national and communal virtue in ending slavery (with little mention of their role in perfecting slavery in the first place). The cult of anti-slavery became an element in that British cultural imperialism which was to characterise much of British behaviour towards the wider world throughout the 19th century.

This was far removed from the world of Ignatius Sancho and the black community of the 1770s and 1780s, a mere two generations earlier. At the time of Sancho's birth, few people questioned the slave system. At the time of his death, it had begun to attract its first serious ethical and economic scrutiny. For much of his life, Sancho lived in a community accustomed to regarding Africans and their slave descendants as mere beasts of burden; destined to be the hewers of wood for the betterment of Europeans. Though he could scarcely have imagined it at the time, Sancho was to become one of the early African voices demanding freedom and equality for blacks scattered throughout the Atlantic diaspora. His life, from slave ship to London shop, provides a reminder of the remarkable upheavals and variety in the life of one African, cast around on both sides of the Atlantic by forces beyond his ken or control. Yet it should also remind us of an alternative world; of Africans demanding their freedom, of rising against the odds, of seeking help and comfort among fellow blacks, and forging important links with sympathetic local whites. From such small, apparently insignificant, events were laid the foundations for the ultimate dissolution of Britain's mighty slave empires. As he wrote his rather grandiloquent letters, Sancho could hardly have imagined the importance we would later attach to his words.

Further Reading

Edwards, P. and P. Rewt (eds) (1994), *The Letters of Ignatius Sancho*, Edinburgh: Edinburgh University Press;

Fryer, P. (1984), *Staying Power: The History of Black People in Britain*, London: Pluto Press;

Walvin, J. (1993), *Black Ivory: A History of British Slavery*, London: Fontana;

Walvin, J. (1996), *Questioning Slavery*, London: Routledge.

Chapter 4

Black Musicians in England: Ignatius Sancho and His Contemporaries

Jane Girdham

Music-making was one of the most popular leisure activities in 18th-century Britain. Gentlemen made sure their daughters learnt to sing and play the harpsichord, and no sophisticated evening's entertainment was complete without music. Amateurs performed at home, in private music clubs, and sometimes next to professional musicians in public venues. Public concerts were held in halls, in pleasure gardens and in theatres, the latter also being a common place for opera performances. Many of the people who formed the audiences at professional concerts were amateurs themselves. They kept music publishers busy printing songs, instrumental pieces, and instruction manuals. A few even composed and published their own music. We know little about them now beyond their printed music unless, like Ignatius Sancho, they were prominent in other spheres. Although Sancho's letters were a best-seller after his death, his music fell into obscurity. Yet without it, we do not have a rounded picture of this black man of letters.

Sancho was by no means the only black musician in 18th-century England; although his amateur status made him one of the least known. A few black musicians made their names as performers, composers and teachers. Music became their way to improve their social and professional standing, often despite the colour of their skin.

Solo instrumentalists made their names on the concert platform. An individual's popularity could be enhanced by some distinctive feature, such as a striking appearance or extreme youth. Child prodigies were always well received, from Mozart in the 1760s to other lesser known figures. Some, like the pianist and composer John Field went on to long professional careers; others soon dropped out of sight (Milligan, 1983, pp. 24–5, 140–1).

One of the most prominent young violinists in London in the 1790s was George Augustus Polgreen Bridgetower (1778–1860), described in a newspaper review of 1790 as 'little Bridgetower, the African' (Milligan, 1983, p. 24)

(Figure 13). His father was West Indian, his mother from eastern Europe. His father had been a servant to Prince Nikolaus Esterházy, the Hungarian aristocrat whose musical court was directed by Joseph Haydn. Indeed Haydn may have taught the young Bridgetower. He came to London with his father in 1789, straight from his début in Paris. In England, Bridgetower *père* adopted a showy pose as an 'African Prince in the Turkish attire' (F. G. E., 1908, p. 303) and callously exploited his son, who eventually secured the patronage of the Prince of Wales (later George IV), himself an amateur cellist. Beethoven composed the 'Kreutzer' Sonata, Op. 47 for Bridgetower (despite a dispute between the two musicians which led Beethoven to alter the dedication), with whom he gave its first performance in Vienna in 1803.

Around the time of Bridgetower's arrival in England another black violinist was trying to establish himself in London. Joseph Bologne, the Chevalier de Saint-Georges (*c.* 1739–1799), was already a prolific composer and well known in Paris, where he had become music director of the Concert des Amateurs in 1773. He was less successful in England where, according to the singer Michael Kelly, Saint-Georges and the violinist Giornovichi 'attempted to carry on concerts by subscription, but they failed' (Kelly, [1826] 1968, p. 339). Saint-Georges, born in Guadeloupe and educated in France by his aristocratic French father, had an unusual dual career. He was also a famous fencer and a soldier, and was better known in England for his fencing matches than for his considerable musical skills.

One of the few other black musicians we know by name was a provincial music teacher, violinist, and composer. Joseph Antonia Emidy (Figure 14) was born in west Africa. He was enslaved and taken to Portugal where he became a violinist at the Lisbon opera house. He was captured in Lisbon by a British naval officer to play dances for his crew, and seven years later was released to settle in Falmouth as a professional musician and teacher. James Silk Buckingham, who took flute lessons from Emidy, failed to bring his music to a wider audience because certain London musicians decided that 'his colour would be so much against him, that there would be a great risk of failure' (Buckingham, [1855] 1973, p. 177).

Not all well-known musicians were so respectable. Billy Waters (died 1823), one-legged 'king of the beggars' and fiddle player, was so well established in London that he played himself on stage in an adaptation of Pierce Egan's *Life in London* and was portrayed in several engravings and broadsheets (Edwards and Walvin, 1983, pp. 163–70).

While some black musicians became professional soloists, others joined military bands, in which they had long been employed as trumpeters and drummers (Farmer, 1950, p. 103). In the last decade or so of the 18th century these musicians were assigned a new role when the British army finally succumbed to the fashion for 'Janissary' instruments in their bands. A group of black musicians would be deliberately set apart from the rest of the players as a 'Janissary' band, distinguished by their skin colour and elaborate costumes, and playing identifiably foreign (Turkish) instruments. This fashion had started on the Continent in the early years of the century when Augustus II of Poland acquired an entire military band from the Turkish sultan. 'Janissary' bands were especially distinguished by percussion sections of bass drum, cymbals, triangle, tambourine, and 'jingling Johnie' (a crescent with bells), whose distinctive sounds soon came to symbolise Turkish music to western European audiences. Composers began to use these instruments to evoke a Turkish atmosphere, most notably Mozart in his opera *Die Entführung aus dem Serail* (The Abduction from the Seraglio) of 1782.

By 1782 the Royal Artillery Band had become the first British regimental band to use Turkish percussion instruments, with a group of bass drum, cymbals and tambourine; other regiments soon followed (Farmer, 1950, p. 45). In Britain the instruments were not played by Turks but by black British musicians dressed flamboyantly in

'Turkish' costume. They quickly gained a reputation for grand gestures and extravagant behaviour:

> Dressed in high turbans, bearskins, or cocked hats, with towering hackle feather plumes, and gaudy coats of many colours, braided and slashed gorgeously and gapingly, they capered rather than marched, and flung their drumsticks and tambourines into the air, adroitly catching them in discreetly measured cadence. Their agility with fingers, arms and legs was only equalled by their perfect time in the music

(Farmer, 1950, p. 46).

Janissary bands reached their height of popularity in Britain in the 1790s, when Haydn made a famous reference to them in his 'Military' Symphony, No. 100, written for the London concert season of 1794. He added a triangle, cymbals and bass drum to the normal orchestra, introducing them with startling effect in the middle of the slow movement. Janissary bands were disbanded early in Queen Victoria's reign, but reminders still survive in the drumstick gestures and leopard-skin aprons of modern military drummers.

Back on the domestic scene, the large black community in London doubtless spawned many an amateur musician, but documentation survives only for the few who found places in the 'white' world, usually through the patronage of some wealthy supporter. Julius Soubise, a Jamaican by birth, was the protégé of the Duchess of Queensberry and, amongst other things, an amateur violinist. His increasingly dissolute life led to a scandal which provoked the Duchess to send him to India in 1778. Sancho's letters criticise Soubise's untrustworthy character, comparing him unfavourably with Sancho's friend Charles Lincoln, another black musician. Lincoln was a ship's bandsman on the boat that Soubise took to India, and was characterised by Sancho as 'honest, trusty, good-natured, and civil'

(Edwards and Rewt, 1994, pp. 35, 95, 154–5, 166–7, 254). Soubise died in India in a riding accident; Lincoln eventually returned home to St. Kitts.

Ignatius Sancho was one of the few Africans in 18th-century England to become a member of the middle class, highly literate and an amateur musician and composer. He was recognised in his lifetime as a man of cultivated taste in various artistic areas, but his legacy of four volumes of published music provides virtually our only information about his musical activities. No copy survives of his *Theory of Music*, which his biographer Jekyll said 'was discussed, published, and dedicated to the Princess Royal' (Edwards and Rewt, 1994, p. 24). His letters give us very few glimpses of his musical activities, just occasional modest remarks such as 'the little dance (which I like because I made it)' (Edwards and Rewt, 1994, p. 115).

Sancho's surviving music consists of one set of songs and three sets of dances, all published over roughly a twelve-year period between 1767 and 1779, and totalling 62 short compositions (Wright, 1981, pp. 3–62). Like most composers before the late 1780s, Sancho did not copyright his editions, so that no copies were assigned to the nine copyright libraries. Few copies of his music survive today. (Their title pages are listed in the bibliography.) Sancho identified himself merely as 'an African' in the first three publications, thus conforming to the habits of many amateur composers by keeping his anonymity (other common descriptions were 'an amateur' and 'a lady'), while at the same time asserting his African heritage. In the last set of dances, Sancho gave his name on the title page, then identified his ethnicity in the title of the final dance. He called it 'Mungo's Delight', after the famous slave character in the opera *The Padlock* (1768) by Charles Dibdin and Isaac Bickerstaffe – 'Mungo' rapidly became slang for 'black man'. Sancho always made his ethnicity clear, using the signature 'Africanus' when writing to newspapers (Edwards and Rewt, 1994, pp. 93, 124), and persistently emphasising his appearance throughout his letters. This constant affirmation of his ethnicity shows a determination to disprove the contemporary opinion that Africans were intellectually inferior to Europeans.

Sancho also indicated his amateur status by having his music published 'for the author', which means he paid for the printing. Again this was the normal method of publication for composers who were not yet established. The title page of the second set of dances names Richard Duke as the printer and music seller. By the time Sancho published his last set in 1779, he had become a public figure and was therefore perhaps less of a financial risk. So thought Samuel and Ann Thompson, the reputable music sellers who published the dances. Sancho dedicated all his published works to close relatives of his third patron, George Brudenell, Duke of Montagu (Wright, 1981, p. xix). But although his dedications suggest he was composing for an aristocratic audience, they certainly do not preclude performance by other groups. For instance, gatherings of black servants would probably have favoured music by a black composer when, as an 18th-century writer reports, they 'entertained themselves with dancing and music, consisting of violins, French horns, and other instruments' where 'all the performers were black' (Wright, 1981, p. xv).

Sancho's music was designed to be performed on social occasions, at dances and at informal domestic recitals. His country dances include instructions for steps. Sancho's instrumental parts are playable by amateurs as well as professionals. In either case most of the players would have been men, because violins, horns and flutes all belonged to a distinctly male preserve. Only the harpsichord (and perhaps the mandolin) were commonly played by women.

The songs are suitable for amateur performers, either women or men. They are printed in the standard two-stave oblong layout of the time, with the vocal part for soprano or tenor. An easy keyboard accompaniment doubles the voice and adds harmonic support. The songs could be performed by a single performer accompanying him- or herself, or by two people.

Sancho's dance music is written in dance forms that were already popular: minuets, English country dances and cotillons (French country dances), some of which he gave colourful English and French titles. A country dance is less a series of specific steps than a choreographed series of movements in a line dance formation. Unlike minuets, country dances can be danced to music in a variety of meters, though in practice they are usually in two to a bar. Sir John Hawkins, a contemporary of Sancho, states that 'for the composition of country-dance tunes no rule is laid down by any of the writers on music, perhaps for this reason, that there is in music no kind of time whatever but may be measured by those motions and gesticulations common in dancing' (Hawkins, [1776] 1963, pp. 705–6n). A minuet, on the other hand, always has three beats in a bar and 'consists of two strains, which, being repeated, are called reprises, each having eight or more bars, but never an odd number' (Hawkins, [1776] 1963, p. 705).

Regular phrasing is just as essential for country dances as for minuets. Sancho's dances all use regular two-bar or four-bar phrases built into short repeated sections. He writes in the popular *galant* or 'pleasing' style of mid-century, with a simple texture and in predominantly major keys. His melodies are tuneful and delicately ornamented; his harmonic style is not adventurous. The dances shown in Figure 15 are representative of Sancho's style. In 'Christmas Eve', two-bar phrases combine into larger repeated sections, and the active melody outlines chords. 'Le douze Decembre' has somewhat broader four-bar phrases, a generally smoother melodic line and more rhythmic variety. Both are harmonically very plain. These titles may indicate when they were originally performed. Other titles seem to be whimsical, while still more may refer to people and places in Sancho's life (Wright, 1981, pp. xxii–iii). His dance 'Lindrindod Lasses', for example, could refer to a visit to Llandrindod Wells by a correspondent of Sancho's, Mrs Cocksedge. Similarly, the dance 'Culford Heath Camp' may be associated either with Sancho's brother-in-law,

John Osborne, who was in the military, or with Mrs Cocksedge, who visited the camp (Edwards and Rewt, 1994, pp. 116, 143).

Sancho's dances can be played by various combinations of instruments. First and second violins, mandolin, German (i.e. transverse) flute, harpsichord, two horns and a bass instrument are listed on the title pages and within the scores. In practice, the dances could have been played on harpsichord alone (as specified for the third set), by a duo of one melody instrument and harpsichord, or by a fuller ensemble that included several melody instruments (violin, flute and mandolin, and any other available instrument), a pair of natural horns and a continuo group of harpsichord with either cello or bassoon.

Sancho's songs are some of his most appealing pieces. They are charming and light in spirit, straightforward and easy to sing. Like other songs being published in increasing numbers in the second half of the 18th century, they were well suited to domestic entertainment.

Sancho's six songs are all in fashionably *galant* style, attractive and within the capabilities of most amateur singers. They are well placed in soprano and tenor ranges (with tenor reading up an octave); there are only a few really high notes, and vocal ornaments are confined to straightforward trills and appoggiaturas.

Sancho showed a wide-ranging poetic taste in his choice of song texts. He set one poem by Shakespeare (from *Measure for Measure*), one by the Greek poet Anacreon in modern translation (Wright, 1981, p. xix), two by David Garrick, and one is anonymous. The last is by 'a young Lady', who may have been an acquaintance. Sancho was also acquainted with Garrick, who was the most famous actor of his time, proprietor of the Theatre Royal Drury Lane, and an author.

Five of the six songs are strophic, with the first verse set to music and subsequent verses written out below to be sung to identical music, like a hymn. The music generally conveys an overall mood rather than illustrating specific words in the poems. In fact, with the exception of the first song of the set, 'The Complaint', the words are often little more than an excuse for a pretty tune. It is clear from the way Sancho broke up the lines of verse, sometimes repeating one short phrase over and over to give direction to the musical shape, that he cared more about musical phrasing than poetic coherence. In 'Sweetest Bard', to a text by Garrick (Figures 16 and 17), he repeats all the lines twice or three times. Like most of the other songs, 'Sweetest Bard' is squarely phrased and harmonically simple. Only in 'The Complaint', the most serious song of the set, does Sancho use musical imagery in direct response to the words, with particular emphasis on 'so sweetly' and colourful harmonies to the words 'but my kisses bring again'.

Sancho never claimed to be a gifted musician, but he obviously felt competent enough to compose and to see his compositions into print. He clearly composed music for real people to sing and dance to, probably people he knew. He kept his pieces simple, within the bounds of his own skills and those of any amateur performer. Within their technical limits, Sancho's compositions work well: they are tuneful, cheerful, easy to understand and easy to remember.

There was never any question of Sancho the African stepping out of the norms of mid-century European musical style, as his education – however he achieved it – had taken place entirely in England. Although Sancho always remembered that his was an adopted culture, his musical compositions are some of the best proof of his assimilation into that culture.

Bibliography

Primary Sources:
Complete list of musical publications by Ignatius Sancho

Minuets, Cotillons & Country Dances for the Violin, Mandolin, German Flute, & Harpsichord Composed by an African Most humbly Inscribed to his Grace Henry Duke of Buccleugh, &c, &c, &c. London. Printed for the Author. [c. 1767].

A Collection of New Songs Composed by An African Humbly Inscribed to the Honble. Mrs James Brudenell by her most humble Devoted & obedient Servant, The Author. [c. 1769].

Minuets &c. &c. for the Violin Mandolin German-Flute and Harpsichord. Compos'd by an African. Book 2d. Humbly Inscribed to the Right Honble. John Lord Montagu of Boughton. London. Printed for the Author and sold by Richd. Duke at his Music Shop near Opposite Great Turn stile Holburn, where may be had Book first. [c. 1770].

Twelve Country Dances for the Year 1779. Set for the Harpsichord By Permission Humbly Dedicated to the Right Honourable Miss North, by her most obedient Servant Ignatius Sancho. London Printed for S and A Thompson No 75 St Pauls Church Yard Price 6d. [1779].

Secondary Sources:

Angelo, H. (1904), *The Reminiscences of Henry Angelo, with Memoirs of His Life, Father and Friends*, [1830], Philadelphia, I, pp. 347–52;

Banat, G. (1990), 'Le Chevalier de Saint-Georges, Man of Music and Gentleman-at-Arms: The Life and Times of an Eighteenth-Century Prodigy', *Black Music Research Journal*, vol. X, pp. 177–212;

Buckingham, J. S. (1973), 'Emidee, A Negro Musician', *The Black Perspective in Music*, vol. I, pp. 175–7;

De Lerma, D-R. (1990), 'Black Composers in Europe: A Works List', *Black Music Research Journal*, vol. X, pp. 275–343;

De Lerma, D-R. (1976), 'The Chevalier de Saint-Georges', *The Black Perspective in Music*, vol. IV, pp. 3–21;

Derr, E. (1980), 'Saint-Georges [Saint-George], Joseph Boulogne, Chevalier de', *The New Grove Dictionary of Music and Musicians*, ed. Stanley Sadie, XVI, pp. 391–2;

E., F. G. (1908), 'George P. Bridgetower and the Kreutzer Sonata', *Musical Times*, vol. IL, pp. 302–8;

Edwards, P. and P. Rewt (eds) (1994), *The Letters of Ignatius Sancho*, Edinburgh: Edinburgh University Press;

Edwards, P. and J. Walvin (1983), *Black Personalities in the Era of the Slave Trade*, Baton Rouge: Louisiana State University;

Farmer, H. G. (1950), *Handel's Kettledrums and Other Papers on Military Music*, London: Hinrichsen;

Hawkins, Sir J. ([1853] 1963), *A General History of the Science and Practice of Music*, 1776, New York: Dover;

Highfill, P. H. Jr., K. A. Burnim and E. A. Langhans (1973–1993), 'Bridgetower, George Augustus Polgreen', in *A Biographical Dictionary of Actors, Actresses, Musicians, Dancers, Managers and Other Stage Personnel in London, 1660–1800*, Carbondale, Ill., vol. II, pp. 332–3;

Kelly, M. ([2nd ed., 1826] 1968), *Reminiscences of Michael Kelly of the King's Theatre and Theatre Royal Drury Lane*, New York: Da Capo Press (1968);

Landon, H. C. R. (1976), *Haydn in England 1791–1795*, pp. 65–7, 256, Bloomington: Indiana University Press;

McGrady, R. (1991), *Music and Musicians in Early Nineteenth-Century Cornwall: The World of Joseph Emidy – Slave, Violinist and Composer*, Exeter: University of Exeter Press;

Milligan, T. (1983), *The Concerto and London's Musical Culture in the Late Eighteenth Century*, Ann Arbor: UMI Research Press;

Papendiek, C. (1887), *Court and Private Life in the Time of Queen Charlotte*, London: Richard Bentley & Son;

Wright, J. (1980), 'George Polgreen Bridgetower: An African Prodigy in England 1789–1799', *Musical Quarterly*, vol. LXVI, pp. 65–82;

Wright, J. R. B. (ed.) (1981), *Ignatius Sancho (1729–1780), An Early African Composer in England: The Collected Editions of His Music in Facsimile*, New York: Garland Publishing Inc.